THE TRINITY

Loraine Boettner

GLH Publishing
Louisville, KY

Originally Published in 1947 as a part of *Studies in Theology*.
Copyright unrenewed, Public Domain

GLH Publishing Reprint, 2019

ISBN:
 Paperback 978-1-948648-80-6
 Epub 978-1-948648-81-3

*Sign up for updates from GLH Publishing
using the link below and receive a free ebook.*
http://eepurl.com/gj9V19

CONTENTS

1. Introduction 1

2. Statement of the Doctrine 8

3. Further Scripture Proof 21

4. The Trinity in the Old Testament 29

5. One Substance, Three Persons 45

6. Meaning of the Terms "Father", "Son", and "Spirit" 54

7. Subordination of the Son and Spirit to the Father 62

8. The Generation of the Son and the Procession of the Holy Spirit 69

9. The Trinity Presents a Mystery but not a Contradiction 75

10. Historical Aspects of the Doctrine 80

11. Practical Importance of the Doctrine 89

1. Introduction

In this chapter we shall attempt to set forth in as clear language as possible the basic truths which the Church holds concerning the doctrine of the Trinity. We shall first present the Scripture evidence on which the doctrine rests and then we shall present the credal statements and formulations that have been set forth by church councils and by individual thinkers as they have applied themselves to the interpretation of that evidence through the two thousand years of the Christian era.

The doctrine of the Trinity is perhaps the most mysterious and difficult doctrine that is presented to us in the entire range of Scripture. Consequently we do not presume to give a full explanation of it. In the nature of the case we can know only as much concerning the inner nature of the Godhead as has been revealed to us in the Scriptures. The tri-personality of God is exclusively a truth of revelation, and one which lies outside the realm of natural reason. Its height and depth and length and breadth are immeasurable by reason of the fact that the finite is dealing with the Infinite. As well might we expect to confine the ocean within a tea-cup as to place a full explanation of the nature of God within the limits of our feeble human minds. It is not our purpose to engage in metaphysical subtleties, nor to speculate on the implications which may be drawn from this doctrine. We do hope, however, that under the guidance of the Holy Spirit we shall be enabled to set forth in a plain simple way, yet as fully as the limitations of our finite minds and language will permit, the truth concerning it, and to guard it against the errors and heresies which have prevailed at one time or another in the history of the Church. While we are not able fully to comprehend the Divine mind, we nevertheless have been created in the image of God and therefore have the right, within limits, to conceive of God according to the analogy of our own nature, and we should be able to grasp enough of this sublime revelation which God has been pleased to give concerning Himself to make a considerable advance in our spiritual growth. Since in the study of this doctrine we are absolutely dependent on revelation (there being nothing else quite similar to or analogous with it in our own consciousness or in the material world), and since the subject of our study is transcendently sacred, that subject being the innermost nature of the infinitely righteous and transcendent God, our attitude should be that of disciples who, with true humility and reverence, are ready to receive implicity whatever God has seen fit to reveal.

Since God is the Creator, Preserver and final Disposer of all things, the One in whom we live and move and have our being, our knowledge of Him must be basic and fundamental to all our knowledge. In answer to the question, "What is God?", the Scriptures reveal Him to us, in the first place, as a rational and righteous Spirit, infinite in His attributes of wisdom, being, power, holiness, justice, goodness, and truth; and in the second place they reveal Him to us as One who exists eternally as three "Persons", these three Persons, however, being one in substance and existing in the most perfect unity of thought and purpose. It is evident, moreover, that if God does thus exist in three Persons, each of whom has His distinctive part in the works of creation, providence, redemption and grace, that fact governs His activity in all spheres of His work and, consequently, the doctrine which treats of the nature of His Person must seriously affect all true theology and philosophy. Doctrines vital to the Christian system, such as those of the Deity and Person of Christ, the Incarnation, the Atonement, etc., are so inextricably interwoven with that of the Tri-unity of God that they cannot be properly understood apart from it.

We should notice that the doctrine of the Trinity is the distinctive mark of the Christian religion, setting it apart from all the other religions of the world. Working without the benefit of the revelations made in Scripture, men have, it is true, arrived at some limited truths concerning the nature and Person of God. The pagan religions, as well as all philosophical speculations, are based on natural religion and can, therefore, rise to no higher conception than that of the unity of God. In some systems we find monotheism with its belief in only one God. In others we find polytheism with its belief in many separate gods. But none of the pagan religions, nor any of the systems of speculative philosophy have ever arrived at a trinitarian conception of God. The fact of the matter is that apart from supernatural revelation there is nothing in human consciousness or experience which can give man the slightest clue to the distinctive God of the Christian faith, the triune, incarnate, redeeming, sanctifying God. Some of the pagan religions have set forth triads of divinities, such as, for instance, the Egyptian triad of Osiris, Isis and Horus, which is somewhat analogous to the human family with father, mother and child; or the Hindu triad of Brahma, Vishnu and Schiva, which in the cycle of pantheistic evolution personifies the creative, preservative and destructive powers of nature; or the triad set forth by Plato, of goodness, intellect and will,—which are not examples of true and proper tri-personality, not real persons who can be addressed and worshipped, but only personifications of the faculties or attributes of God. None of these systems have anything in common with the Christian doctrine of the Trinity except the notion of "threeness".

Before undertaking the more detailed study of the doctrine of the Trinity it may be well to remind ourselves that man's knowledge of God has been progressive. The most general revelation of the existence of God has been given through nature and is therefore common to all men. The existence of God is an intuitive truth universally accepted by the unprejudiced mind. Man knows himself to be dependent and responsible, and therefore posits the One on whom he is dependent and to whom he is responsible. He attributes to this One in an eminent degree all of the good qualities which he finds in himself, and thus comes to know God as a personal Spirit, infinite, eternal, and perfect in His attributes.

The Second stage in the revelation concerning the nature and attributes of God was that given through the Old Testament period. There a great advance is made over the revelation given through man's intuition and through nature, and God is disclosed as particularly the God of grace and the redeemer of sinners. The third stage, the one in which at present we are particularly interested, is that given in the New Testament in which God is represented as existing in a trinity of Persons, each of whom performs a distinctive part in the works of creation, providence, and redemption. As Dr. Warfield has pointed out:

"The elements of the plan of salvation are rooted in the mysterious nature of the Godhead, in which there coexists a trinal distinction of persons with absolute unity of essence; and the revelation of the Trinity was accordingly incidental to the execution of this plan of salvation, in which the Father sent the Son to be the propitiation for sin, and the Son, when He returned to the glory which He had with the Father before the world was, sent the Spirit to apply His redemption to men. The disclosure of this fundamental fact of the divine nature, therefore, lagged until the time had arrived for the actual working out of the long-promised redemption; and it was accomplished, first of all in fact rather than in word, by the actual appearance of God the Son on earth and the subsequent manifestations of the Spirit, who was sent forth to act as His representative in His absence."[1]

We believe that the cosmological, teleological, ontological, and moral arguments for the existence of God are valid for any one with an open and unprejudiced mind. Perhaps they will not convince a rationalist or an atheist, but at present we are not particularly concerned with that class of persons. That theism alone is capable of solving the riddle of the universe is the firm conviction of present day scientific and philosophical thought as we have it set forth in the writings of the most outstanding leaders in these fields, such as Eddington, Jeans, Millikan, Whitehead, Hocking, Brightman, etc. The materialistic concept which held almost undisputed sway a few decades ago has been replaced with

---

1 *Studies in Theology*, p. 113

the idea that behind all that we see there is a personal God who is the Creator and Sustainer of the universe.

The present writer assumes that his readers are convinced theists. Others could hardly be expected to have an interest in theology, much less to be concerned about the doctrine of the Trinity. The psalmist gave the divine appraisal of Atheism in the words, "The fool hath said in his heart. There is no God" (14:1). As a recent writer has pointed out, Atheism is "the very quintessence of absurdity, folly raised to the *nth* degree. In view of the manifold proofs of His power and wisdom on every hand, it is hard to see how any open mind can deny the existence of a Supreme Being who rules over all. To maintain that this far-flung universe is the result of an accidental juxtaposition of atoms, a fortuitous confluence of cosmic forces, is a hypothesis too nonsensical for refutation. As has been pointed out more than once, as well expect a million monkeys banging away on typewriters accidentally to produce a *Paradise Lost*. An atheistic explanation of the origin of the world (the sum total of all that is) calls for an immeasurably greater credulity than the tenets of Theism. If there be no God the cosmos is a hopeless riddle."[2]

But while it is so widely recognized that Theism alone offers an adequate explanation of the universe, the fact remains that many theists who firmly believe in the existence of a personal God deny just as strongly that there is a plurality of persons in the Godhead as is set forth in the trinitarian faith. In the Christian doctrine of the Trinity they see only tritheism, or some one of the myriad varieties of polytheism which have been so common in both ancient and modern times. They look upon it as an absurdity or as a contradiction

---

[2] Dr. C. Norman Bartlett, *The Triune God*, p. 36

of terms, and are never tired of asserting that if God is one He cannot be three. But when we give more careful thought to the theistic problem we find that the absurdity and irrationality lie on their side of the fence, and that the conception of God as an eternally lonely, solitary person is utterly out of the question. And while we do not go so far as to say that the personality of God necessarily implies the doctrine of the Trinity, we do believe that the personal traits of love, honour, fellowship, trust, sympathy, etc., cannot flower forth in their full beauty and fragrance unless there are objective personal relationships, and that this is true of Deity as well as of humanity.

The theory that God is superpersonal is, of course, an absurdity. In the nature of the case Divine personality is an infinitely greater thing than human personality; but the only alternative to a personal God is an impersonal God. And when we assert that God is impersonal we assert the primary tenet of atheism. If God exists. He must be personal. We cannot worship the Principle of the Absolute, nor hold communion with a Cosmic Power; and to assert that God is super-personal is but to deceive ourselves with a high-sounding phrase.

2. Statement of the Doctrine

Assuming that Theism is the accepted form of belief, and that God is personal, we would state the doctrine of the Trinity under the following heads:

I. There Is But One Living and True God

One of the most common objections alleged against the doctrine of the Trinity is that it involves tritheism, or a belief in three Gods. The fact of the matter, however, is that it stands unalterably opposed to tritheism as well as to every other form of polytheism. Scripture, reason and conscience are in perfect agreement that there is but one self-existent, eternal, supreme Being in whom all of the divine attributes or perfections inhere and from whom they cannot be separated. That both the Old and the New Testament do teach the unity of God is clearly set forth in the following verses:

"Hear, O Israel: Jehovah our God is one Jehovah" (Deut. 6:4). "Thus saith Jehovah, the King of Israel, and his Redeemer, Jehovah of hosts: I am the first, and I am the last; and beside me there is no God" (Isa. 44:6). The Decalogue, which is the foundation of the moral and religious code of Christianity, as well as of Judaism, has as its first and greatest commandment, "Thou shalt have no other gods before me" (Exod. 20:3). "I and the Father are one," said Jesus (John 10:30). "Thou believest that God is one; thou doest well" (Jas. 2:19). "We know that no idol is anything in the world, and that there is no God but one" (1 Cor. 8:4). There is but "one Lord, one faith, one baptism, one God and Father of all, who is over all, and through all, and in all" (Eph. 4:5, 6). "I am the Alpha and the Omega, the first and the last, the beginning and the end" (Rev. 22:13). From Genesis to Revelation God is declared to be one.

That the universe is a unit is the settled conclusion of modern science and philosophy; and with this, of course, goes the corollary that the God who created it and who rules it is One. Astronomers tell us, for instance, that the same principles which govern in our solar system are also found in the millions of stars which are trillions of miles away. Physicists analyze the light that comes from the sun and from the distant stars and tell us that not only are the same elements, such as iron, carbon, oxygen, etc., which are found on the earth also found on them, but that these elements are found in practically the same proportion as here. From the law of gravitation we learn that every material object in the universe attracts every other material object with a force which is directly proportional to their masses and inversely proportional to the square of the distance between their centers. Hence every grain of sand in the desert and on the sea-shore is linked up with every sun in the universe. The sluggish earth mounts upward to meet the falling snowflake. The microscope reveals marvels just as wonderful as those revealed by the telescope, and everywhere it is the same unified system.

Certainly the Unitarians have no monopoly on the doctrine of the unity of God. Trinitarians hold this just as definitely. The unity of God is one of the basic postulates of theism, and no system can possibly be true which teaches otherwise.

II. While God in His Innermost Nature Is One, He, Nevertheless, Exists as Three Persons

The best concise definition of the doctrine of the Trinity, so far as we are aware, is that found in the Westminster Shorter Catechism: "There are three persons within the Godhead; the Father, the Son and the Holy Ghost; and these three are one God, the same in substance, equal in power and glory." We would prefer, however, to use the term "Spirit" rather than "Ghost," since a ghost is commonly understood to be a spirit that once had a body but lost it, and the Holy Spirit has never possessed a body of any kind.

We have seen that the Scriptures teach that there is but one true and living God. They teach with equal clearness that this one God exists as three distinct Persons, as Father, Son, and Holy Spirit:

(*a*) The Father is God: "To us there is one God, the Father, of whom are all things" (1 Cor. 8:6). "Paul, an apostle...through Jesus Christ, and God the Father" (Gal. 1:1). "There is...one God and Father of all" (Eph. 4:6). "At that season Jesus answered and said, I thank thee, O Father, Lord of heaven and earth..." (Matt. 11:25). "For him (the Son) the Father, even God, hath sealed" (John 6:27). "According to the foreknowledge of God the Father" (1 Pet. 1:2). "That every tongue should confess that Jesus Christ is Lord, to the glory of God the Father" (Phil. 2:11). "I ascend unto my Father and your Father, and my God and your God" (John 20:17). "But the hour cometh, and now is, when the true worshippers shall worship the Father in spirit and truth" (John 4:23). Jesus prayed to God the Father (Mark 14:36; John 11:41; 17:11, etc.).

(*b*) The Son is God: "Christ...who is over all, God blessed for ever" (Rom. 9:5). "For in Him (Christ) dwelleth all the fulness of the Godhead bodily" (Col. 2:9). "Thomas answered and said unto him, My Lord and my God" (John 20:28). "I and the Father are one" (John 10:30). "Looking for the blessed hope and appearing of the glory of the great God and our Saviour Jesus Christ" (Titus 2:13). "Thou art the Christ, the Son of the living God" (Matt. 16:16). Christ assumed power over the Sabbath, and "called God His own Father, making Himself equal with God" (John 5:18). He assumed the prerogatives of God in forgiving sins (Mark 2:5). "In the beginning was the Word, and the Word was with God, and the Word was God" (John 1:1).

The attributes which can be ascribed only to God are ascribed to Christ: Holiness—"Thou art the Holy One of God" (John 6:69); "Him who knew no sin," (2 Cor. 5:21); "Which of you convicteth me of sin?" (John 8:46); "Holy, guileless, undefiled, separate from sinners" (Heb. 7:26). Eternity—"In the beginning was the Word" (John 1:1); "Before Abraham was born, I am" (John 8:58); "But of the Son he saith, Thy throne, O God, is for ever and ever" (Heb. 1:8); "The glory which I had with thee before the world was" (John 17:5). Life—"In Him was life" (John 1:4); "I am the way, and the truth, and the life: no one cometh unto the Father but by me" (John 14:6); "I am the resurrection and the life" (John 11:25). Immutability—"Jesus Christ is the same yesterday and today, yea and for ever" (Heb. 13:8), "They (the heavens) shall perish; but thou continuest.... They shall be changed: but thou art the same" (Heb. 1:11, 12). Omnipotence—"All authority hath been given unto me in heaven and on earth" (Matt. 28:18); "The Lord God, who is and who was and who is to come, the Almighty" (Rev. 1:8). Omniscience—"Thou knowest all things" (John 16:30); "Jesus knowing their thoughts" (Matt. 9:4);

"Jesus knew from the beginning who they were that believed not, and who it was that should betray Him" (John 6:64); "In whom are all the treasures of wisdom and knowledge hidden" (Col. 2:3). Omnipresence—"I am with you always" (Matt. 28:20); "The fulness of him that filleth all in all" (Eph. 1:23). Creation—"All things were made through him; and without him was not anything made that hath been made" (John 1:3); "The world was made through him" (John 1:10); "For in him were all things created, in the heavens and upon the earth, things visible and things invisible, whether thrones or dominions or principalities or powers; all things have been created through him, and unto him; and he is before all things, and in him all things consist" (Col. 1:16, 17); "Upholding all things by the word of his power" (Heb. 1:3). Raising the dead—"And he (God the Father) gave him (Christ the Son) authority to execute judgment...for the hour cometh in which all that are in the tombs shall hear his voice, and shall come forth; they that have done good, unto the resurrection of life; and they that have done evil, unto the resurrection of judgment" (John 5:27–29). Judgment of all men—"But when the Son of man shall come in his glory, and all the angels with him, then shall he sit on the throne of his glory: and before him shall be gathered all the nations: and he shall separate them one from another, as the shepherd separateth the sheep from the goats; and he shall set the sheep on his right hand, and the goats on the left. Then shall the King say unto them on his right hand, Come, ye blessed of my Father, inherit the kingdom prepared for you from the foundation of the world.... And he shall say also unto them on the left hand, Depart from me, ye cursed, into the eternal fire, which is prepared for the devil and his angels.... And these shall go away into eternal punishment: but the righteous into eternal life" (Matt. 25:31–46). Prayer and worship are to be directed to Christ—"If ye shall ask anything in my name, that will I do" (John 14:14); "He was parted from them, and was carried up into heaven. And they worshipped him" (Luke 24:51, 52); "Stephen, calling upon the Lord, and saying, Lord Jesus, receive my spirit" (Acts 7:59); all are to "honor the Son, even as they honor the Father. He that honoreth not the Son honoreth not the Father that sent him" (John 5:23); "Believe on the Lord Jesus, and thou shalt be saved" (Acts 16:31); "Let all the angels of God worship him" (Heb. 1:6); "That in the name of Jesus every knee should bow…and that every tongue should confess that Jesus Christ is Lord, to the glory of God the Father" (Phil. 2:10, 11); "Our Lord and Saviour Jesus Christ" (2 Pet. 3:18); "Jesus Christ, to whom be the glory for ever and ever" (Heb. 13:21;—and when we compare these verses with statements such as we have in Isaiah, "Look unto me and be ye saved, all the ends of the earth; for I am God, and there is none else" (45:22), and Jeremiah, "Thus saith Jehovah, Cursed is the man that trusteth in man and maketh flesh his arm" (17:5), we are faced with this dilemma: either the Christian doctrine of the Trinity must be true, or the Scriptures are self-contradictory; either the Scriptures recognize more Gods than one, or Christ, together with the Father and the Holy Spirit is that one God.

All of these ascriptions of holiness, eternity, life, immutability, omnipotence, omniscience, omnipresence, creation, providence, raising the dead, judgment of all men, prayer and worship due to Christ, most clearly teach His Deity. Such attitudes of mind if directed toward a creature would be idolatrous.

(c) The Holy Spirit is God: "Peter said, Ananias, why hath Satan filled thy heart to lie to the Holy Spirit?... Thou has not lied unto men, but unto God" (Acts 5:3, 4); "For who among men knoweth the things of a man, save the spirit of the man, which is in him? even so the things of God none knoweth, save the Spirit of God" (1 Cor. 2:11); "But when the Comforter is come, whom I will send unto you from the Father, even the Spirit of truth, which proceedeth from the Father, he shall bear witness of me" (John 15:26). In the Baptismal Formula, "Go ye therefore, and make disciples of all the nations, baptizing them in the name of the Father, and of the Son, and of the Holy Spirit" (Matt. 28:19), and in the Apostolic Benediction, "The grace of the Lord Jesus Christ, and the love of God, and the communion of the Holy Spirit, be with you all" (2 Cor. 13:14), the Holy Spirit is placed on a plane of absolute equality with the Father and the Son as Deity and is regarded equally with them as the source of all power and blessing.

There are many, even among professedly Christian people, who have no higher conception of the Holy Spirit than that of an impersonal, mysterious, supernatural power or influence of God. It is true that in the Old Testament, where the emphasis was upon the unity of God, the references to the Spirit, while not incapable of being applied to a distinct person, were more generally understood to designate simply God's power or influence. But in the more advanced revelation of the New Testament the distinct personality of the Holy Spirit is clearly seen. No longer can He be looked upon as merely a divine power or influence, but as a divine Person. Some people, even among those in the Christian Churches, because they are very thoughtless, speak of

2. STATEMENT OF THE DOCTRINE

the Holy Spirit as *it*, when a little reflection would show them that the proper term is *He* or *Him*.

That the Holy Spirit is a Person is clearly taught in the following verses: "The Spirit said unto Philip, Go near, and join thyself to this chariot" (Acts 8:29). "The Spirit said unto him (Peter). Behold, three men seek thee. But arise, and get thee down, go with them, nothing doubting: for I have sent them" (Acts 10:19, 20). "The Holy Spirit said, separate me Barnabas and Saul for the work whereunto I have called them" (Acts 13:2). "The Holy Spirit shall teach you in that very hour what ye ought to say" (Luke 12:12). "When he, the Spirit of truth, is come, he shall guide you into all the truth: for he shall not speak from himself; but what things soever he shall hear, these shall he speak: and he shall declare unto you the things that are to come. He shall glorify me: for he shall take of mine, and shall declare it unto you" (John 16:13, 14). "And I will pray the Father, and he shall give you another Comforter, that he may be with you for ever, even the Spirit of truth: whom the world cannot receive; for it beholdeth him not, neither knoweth him: ye know him; for he abideth with you, and shall be in you" (John 14:16, 17),—here the Holy Spirit is called a "Comforter" (marginal reference Advocate), that is, one called to stand by our side as our Guide, Teacher, Instructor, Sponsor; and in the nature of the case, therefore, He must be a Person. In a parallel passage Christ is similarly spoken of,—"We have an Advocate with the Father, Jesus Christ the righteous" (1 John 2:1) "The spirit Himself maketh intercession for us with groanings which cannot be uttered" (Rom. 8:26). "Grieve not the Holy Spirit of God" (Eph. 4:30). "He that hath an ear, let him hear what the Spirit saith to the churches" (Rev. 2:17). "Every sin and blasphemy shall be forgiven unto men; but the blasphemy against the Spirit shall not be forgiven. And whosoever shall speak a word against the Son of man, it shall be forgiven him; but whosoever shall speak against the Holy Spirit, it shall not be forgiven him, neither in this world, nor in that which is to come" (Matt. 12:31, 32)—the language here used implies that it is impossible to commit a sin against a more divine personage than the Holy Spirit, that of all possible sins the sin against the Holy Spirit is the worst, both in its nature and consequences, and thus implies His eternal dignity and Deity.

Words which in the Old Testament are ascribed to God are in the New Testament more specifically said to have been spoken by the Holy Spirit,—compare Jer. 31:33, 34 with Heb. 10:15–17; Ps. 95:7–11 with Heb. 3:7–11; Isa. 6:9, 10 with Acts 28:25–28. In the Old Testament we read that the Holy Spirit brought order out of the primeval chaos (Gen. 1:2); and He strove to lead the ante-diluvians in the ways of righteousness (Gen. 6:3); He equipped certain men to become prophets (Num. 11:26, 29); He instructed the Israelites as a people (Neh. 9:20); He came upon Isaiah and equipped him to be a prophet (61:1), and caused Ezekiel to go and preach to those of the captivity (3:12, 15). In the New Testament the miracle of the virgin birth of Christ was wrought through His power (Luke 1:35); He descended on Jesus at the baptism and equipped Him for the public ministry (Matt. 3:16); He was promised as a Comforter and Teacher to the disciples (John 16:7–13); He came upon the disciples on the day of Pentecost and equipped them to be world missionaries (Acts 2:1–42); He kept Paul from going in one direction and sent him in another (Acts 16:6–10); He equips different individuals with different gifts and talents (1 Cor. 12:4–31); He performs the supernatural work of regenerating the souls of men (Titus 3:5, John 3:5); He inspired the prophets and apostles so that what they spoke or wrote in God's name was truly His word to the people (2 Pet. 1:20, 21); in the works of regeneration and sanctification He applies to the heart of each of the Lord's people the objective redemption which was wrought out by Christ, and in general He directs the affairs of the advancing Church. He is thus set forth as the Author of order and beauty in the physical world, and of faith and holiness in the spiritual world.

Throughout the Scriptures the Holy Spirit is thus set forth as a distinct Person, with a mind, will and power of His own. Baptism is administered in His name. He is constantly associated with two other Persons, the Father and the Son, whose distinct personalities are recognized,—a phenomenon which could lead only to confusion if He too were not a distinct Person. The personal pronouns, "He," "Him," "I," and "Me," are applied to Him, pronouns which can be used intelligently only when applied to a person. They occur so repeatedly through the prose narratives and cannot be set aside as a tendency to personify an impersonal force. That two and two make four does not appear more clear and conclusive than that the Holy Spirit is a living Agent, working with consciousness, will and power.

After the personality of the Holy Spirit is established there are but few who will deny His Deity. It is certain that He is not a creature, and consequently those who admit His personality accept His Deity readily enough. Most of the heretical sects that have maintained that Christ was a mere man have, in accordance with that, maintained that the Spirit was only a power or influence. This was the opinion held by the Gnostics and Socinians, as well as that held by present-day Unitarians and rationalists.

That there should be any doubt at all concerning the personality of the Spirit may seem strange; and yet, as Dr. A. H. Strong has pointed out:

"It is noticeable that in Scripture there is no obtrusion of the Holy Spirit's personality, as if He (the One who inspired the prophets as they wrote) desired to draw attention to Himself. The Holy Spirit shows not Himself, but Christ. Like John the Baptist, He is a mere voice, and so an example to Christian preachers, who are themselves 'made...sufficient as ministers...of the spirit' (2 Cor. 3:6). His leading is therefore often unperceived; He so joins Himself to us that we infer His presence only from the new and holy exercises of our own minds; He continues to work in us even when His presence is ignored and His purity is outraged by our sins."[3]

III. THE TERMS "FATHER," "SON" AND "HOLY SPIRIT" DESIGNATE DISTINCT PERSONS WHO ARE OBJECTIVE TO EACH OTHER

The terms Father, Son and Spirit do not merely designate the different relations which God assumes toward His creatures. They are not analogous to the terms Creator, Preserver and Benefactor, which do express such relations, but are the proper names of different subjects who are distinct from one another as one person is distinct from another. That this is true is clear from the following personal relations which they bear toward each other:

---

3 *Systematic Theology*, p. 324

(*a*) They mutually use the pronouns I, thou, he and him when speaking to or of each other. "This is my beloved Son, in whom I am well pleased; hear ye him" (Matt. 17:5). "Father, the hour is come; glorify thy Son, that the Son may glorify thee" (John 17:1). "I came out from the Father, and am come into the world: again, I leave the world, and go unto the Father" (John 16:28). "When he, the Spirit of truth, is come, he shall guide you into all the truth: for he shall not speak from himself: but what things soever he shall hear, these shall he speak: and he shall declare unto you the things that are to come" (John 16:13).

(*b*) The Father loves the Son, and the Son loves the Father. The Spirit glorifies the Son. "The Father loveth the Son, and hath given all things into his hand" (John 3:35). "I have kept my Father's commandments, and abide in his love" (John 15:10). "He (the Holy Spirit) shall glorify me; for he shall take of mine, and shall declare it unto you" (John 16:14).

(*c*) The Son prays to the Father. "And now, Father, glorify thou me with thine own self with the glory which I had with thee before the world was" (John 17:5). "And I will pray the Father, and he shall give you another Comforter, that he may be with you for ever" (John 14:16).

(*d*) The Father sends the Son, and the Father and the Son send the Holy Spirit who acts as their Agent. "He that receiveth you receiveth me, and he that receiveth me receiveth him that sent me" (Matt. 10:40). "As thou didst send me into the world" (John 17:18). "And this is life eternal, that they should know thee the only true God, and him whom thou didst send, even Jesus Christ" (John 17:3). "But the Comforter, even the Holy Spirit, whom the Father will send in my name, he shall teach you all things, and bring to your remembrance all that I said unto you" (John 14:26). "It is expedient for you that I go away; for if I go not away, the Comforter will not come unto you; but if I go, I will send him unto you" (John 16:7).

Thus we see that the Persons within the Godhead are so distinct that each can address the others, each can love the others, the Father sends the Son, the Father and the Son send the Spirit, the Son prays to the Father, and we can pray to each of them. They act and are acted upon as subject and object, and each has a particular work to perform. We say they are distinct persons, for a person is one who can say I, who can be addressed as thou, and who can act and be the object of action.

The doctrine of the Trinity, then, is but the synthesis of these facts. When we have said these three things,— that there is but one God, that the Father and the Son and the Spirit is each God, and that the Father and the Son and the Spirit is each a distinct Person,—we have enunciated the doctrine of the Trinity in its fulness. This is the form in which it is found in the Scriptures, and it is also the form in which it has entered into the faith of the Church.

3. Further Scripture Proof

While there is no single passage in Scripture which sets forth the doctrine of the Trinity in formal, credal statement, there are numerous passages in which the three Persons are mentioned in such a manner as to exhibit at once their unity and their distinctness. Most important of these is the Great Commission given in Matthew 28:19, in which baptism is commanded "in the name of the Father and of the Son and of the Holy Spirit." In this, the initiatory rite of the Christian religion, the doctrine of the Trinity is purposely set forth in such a manner as to keep it before the minds of the people as a cardinal doctrine of the faith. "What we witness here," says Dr. Warfield, "is the authoritative announcement of the Trinity as the God of Christianity by its Founder, in one of the most solemn of His recorded declarations. Israel had worshipped the one only true God under the Name of Jehovah; Christians are to worship the same one only and true God under the Name of 'the Father, and the Son, and the Holy Spirit.' This is the distinguishing characteristic of Christians; and that is as much as to say that the doctrine of the Trinity is, according to our Lord's own apprehension of it, the distinctive mark of the religion which He founded." (*Biblical Doctrines*, p. 155).

The Apostolic Benediction—"The grace of the Lord Jesus Christ, and the love of God, and the communion of the Holy Spirit, be with you all" (2 Cor. 13:14), which is a prayer addressed to Christ for His grace, to the Father for His love, and to the Holy Spirit for His fellowship—is designed to serve the same purpose. In this formula, as in that of baptism, the divinity, and consequently the equality, of each of the persons in the Godhead is taken for granted; and no other interpretation is rationally possible except that which the Church has held down through the ages, namely, that God exists in three Persons and that these three are one in substance, equal in power and glory.

In the account of our Lord's baptism we find as clear teaching concerning the reality of the Trinity as any one can reasonably ask for,—Christ the Son stood there in human form and was visible to all the people, the voice of God the Father spoke from heaven, saying, "This is my beloved Son, in whom I am well pleased," find the descent of the Holy Spirit upon Christ was seen as that of a dove (Matt. 3:16, 17).

In the announcement of the birth of Jesus three divine Persons came into view: "And the angel answered and said unto her, The Holy Spirit shall come upon thee, and the power of the Most High shall overshadow thee: wherefore also the holy thing which is begotten shall be called the Son of God" (Luke 1:35). Here we read of the coming of the Holy Spirit, of the power of the Most High, and are told that the Child is to be known as the Son of God. Also, in the parallel account of Matthew 1:18–23 the three persons of the Trinity are named.

The distinction between the Father and the Son and the Holy Spirit is announced by Jesus when He says: "But when the Comforter is come, whom I will send unto you from the Father, He shall bear witness of me" (John 15:26).

In the final discourse and prayer (John, chs. 14–17), Christ spoke to and of the Father and promised to send another Comforter, the Holy Spirit, who would guide, teach, and inspire the disciples. Here again the personality and Deity of the Father, Son and Holy Spirit are recognized with special clearness.

The teaching of Jesus is, of course, trinitarian throughout. In accordance with the Hebrew idea of sonship,—that whatever the father is, that the son is also,—He claimed to be the Son of God (Matt. 9:27; 24:36; Mark 8:31; Luke 10:22; John 9:35–37; 11:4); and the Jews, with exact appreciation of His meaning, understood Him to claim that He was "equal with God" (John 5:18), or, to put it more briefly, they understood Him to claim that He was "God" (John 10:33). He claims that He knows the Father and that the Father knows Him with perfect mutual knowledge: "All things have been delivered unto me of my Father: and no one knoweth who the Son is, save the Father; and who the Father is, save the Son, and he to whomsoever the Son willeth to reveal him" (Luke 10:22; also Matt. 11:27). The title, "Son of God," in such a sense that it involves absolute community with God the Father in knowledge and power, is attributed to Him and accepted by Him (Matt. 8:29; 14:33; 27:40, 43, 54; Mark 3:11; Luke 4:41; 22:70; John 1:34, 49; 11:27). But while He thus asserts that His eternal home is in the depths of the Divine Being, He sets forth in equally clear language His distinctness from the Father: "Jesus said unto them, If God were your Father, ye would love me: for I came forth and am come from God; for neither have I come of myself, but he sent me" (John 8:42). And to His disciples He said: "In that day ye shall ask in my name: and I say not unto you, that I will pray the Father for you; for the Father himself loveth you, because ye have loved me, and have believed that I came forth from the Father. I came out from the Father, and am come into the world; again, I leave the world, and go unto the Father" (John 16:26–28).

Hence our primary reason for believing the doctrine of the Trinity is, as we have stated elsewhere, not because of any general tendency of human thinking to go in that direction, nor because of any analogies in nature, but only because it is a clearly revealed doctrine of the Bible. For those who accept the authority of the Scriptures the evidence is conclusive. We do not here attempt to argue with those who deny that authority, but refer them to the Christian doctrine of the Inspiration of the Scriptures. Unless we are agreed that the Scriptures are an authoritative revelation from God, it is useless to argue over the doctrine of the Trinity. The Christian finds the proofs for the trust-worthiness of the Bible so convincing that he is compelled to accept its teaching concerning the Trinity even though his finite mind is not able to comprehend its full meaning.

Yet while it is true that the evidence for the doctrine of the Trinity is found in the Bible, it is also true that, as in the case of the other doctrines in the Christian system, there is no place where this doctrine is set forth in a complete and systematic form. The different elements of the doctrine, such as the unity of God, the true and equal Deity of the Father, Son and Holy Spirit, their distinct personality, the relationship which they bear to each other, to the Church, and to the world, etc., while expressed most clearly in the New Testament are found scattered through all parts of the Bible from the first chapter of Genesis to the last of Revelation. It is only by proving these elements separately, as we have attempted to do, that the truth of the whole doctrine is most satisfactorily brought out. The doctrine is given in Scripture, not in formulated definition, but in fragmentary allusions; and it is only as we assemble the *disjecta membra* into their organic unity that we are able to grasp its true meaning. It lies in Scripture as it were in solution, and comes into clear view only when it is crystallized out from its solvent. The Bible is not a work on Systematic Theology, but only the quarry out of which the stone for such a temple can be obtained. Instead of giving us a formal statement of a theological system it gives us a mass of raw materials which are to be organized and systematized and worked up into their organic relations. Nowhere, for instance, do we find a formal statement of the doctrine of the Inspiration of the Scriptures, or of the sovereignty of God, or of the Person of Christ. The Bible gives us an account of the creation of the world and of man, of the entrance of sin, and of God's purpose to redeeem man from sin. It tells particularly of God's merciful dealings with one group of people, the Israelites, and of the founding of Christianity; and the doctrinal facts are given with but little regard to their logical relations. These doctrinal facts therefore need to be classified and arranged into a logical system and thus transformed into theology. That the material in the Bible is not arranged in a theological system is in accordance with God's procedure in other realms. He has not given us a fully developed system of biology, astronomy, economics, or politics. We simply find the unorganized facts in nature and experience, and are left to develop them into a system as best we may. And since the doctrines are not thus presented in a systematic and formal way it is, of course, much easier for varied and false interpretations to arise.

That even in the New Testament the doctrine of the Trinity is not set forth with anything even approaching systematic treatment, but rather in the form of incidental allusions, may occasion some surprise. But while not presenting the doctrine with argumentative reasoning, nor in creedal statements, the New Testament everywhere assumes it; and the unstudied naturalness and simplicity with which it is given makes it all the more impressive and illuminating. We find not merely a text here and there, but such a wealth of trinitarian implications that, as Dr. Bartlett says:

"They blossom forth everywhere in such profusion that the reverent and unprejudiced reader seeking light upon this subject is troubled, not by a paucity of proof texts, but by an embarrassment of riches."[4]

Dr. Warfield points out that the whole book is saturated with Trinitarianism:

"Jesus Christ and the Holy Spirit are the fundamental proof of the doctrine of the Trinity. This is as much as to say that all the evidence of whatever kind, and from whatever source derived, that Jesus Christ is God manifested in the flesh, and that the Holy Spirit is a Divine Person, is just so much evidence for the doctrine of the Trinity; and when we go to the New Testament for evidence of the Trinity we are to seek it, not merely in the scattered illusions to the Trinity as such, numerous and instructive as they are, but primarily in the whole mass of evidence which the New Testament provides of the Deity of Christ and the Divine personality of the Holy Spirit. When we have said this, we have said in effect that the whole mass of the New Testament is evidence for the Trinity. For the New Testament is saturat-

---

4 *The Triune God*, p. 22

ed with evidence of the Deity of Christ and the Divine personality of the Holy Spirit."[5]

That a doctrine which to us is so difficult should, even in the hands of a people who had become fiercely monotheistic, take its place silently and imperceptibly among accepted Christian truths without struggle and without controversy, is certainly one of the most remarkable phenomena in the history of human thought. We have not far to seek, however, for the explanation. Marvellous developments had taken place between the closing of the Old Testament and the opening of the New. To quote Dr. Warfield again:

"It may carry us a little way to remark, as it has been customary to remark since the time of Gregory of Nazianzus, that it was the task of the Old Testament revelation to fix firmly in the minds and hearts of the people of God the great fundamental truth of the unity of the Godhead; and it would have been dangerous to speak to them of the plurality within this unity until this task had been fully accomplished. The real reason for the delay in the revelation of the Trinity, however, is grounded in the secular development of the redemptive purpose of God; the times were not ripe for the revelation of the Trinity in the unity of the Godhead until the fulness of the time had come for God to send forth His Son unto redemption, and His Spirit unto sanctification. The revelation in word must needs wait upon the revelation in fact, to which it brings its necessary explanation, no doubt, but from which it derives its own entire significance and value. The revelation of a Trinity in the Divine unity as a mere abstract truth without relation to manifested fact, and without significance to the development of the kingdom of God, would have

---

[5] *Biblical Doctrines*, p. 146

been foreign to the whole method of the Divine procedure as it lies exposed to us in the pages of Scripture."[6]

The revelation that God exists in three Persons, as Father, Son and Holy Spirit, is, in fact, the only basis on which the Christian doctrine of redemption can be intelligently set forth. Hence the revelation concerning the plurality of Persons in the Godhead is not given for the mere purpose of presenting something which shall be puzzling and inscrutable to human minds, but as a necessary step in the much fuller revelation concerning the plan of salvation. The incarnation of God the Son and the outpouring of God the Holy Spirit at Pentecost marked two tremendous advances in the divine plan. The revelation of the Trinity was incidental to the fuller development of the plan of salvation, and at the time of the writing of the New Testament books the doctrine was already the common property of Christian believers. Hence in speaking and writing to one another they assumed this common trinitarian consciousness rather than instructed one another about something concerning which there was no disagreement, and the result is that we find the doctrine everywhere pre-supposed, presented in the form of allusion rather than in express teaching.

---

[6] *Biblical Doctrines*, p. 145

4. The Trinity in the Old Testament

In regard to all of the great doctrines of the Bible we find that revelation has been progressive. What is only intimated at first is set forth clearly and fully as time goes on. The obscure hint in the Old Testament is found to coincide perfectly with the fuller revelations in the New. As with our physical eyesight God does not cause the sun to rise with a sudden flash, lest such strong and glorious light should blind us, so He has also borne with our immature spiritual eyesight; He did not at first manifest Himself in the wonderful personality of the Messiah, the sun of Righteousness, and in the personality of the Holy Spirit, but revealed Himself gradually, precept upon precept, line upon line, here a little, there a little, until our understanding was prepared to receive the whole truth. Since the doctrine of the Trinity is one which arises out of the completed redemption as it is presented to us in the New Testament and cannot be intelligently comprehended apart from that redemption, we should not expect to find it set forth with any clearness in the Old Testament. And yet, if the doctrine is a vital and necessary part of the Christian system we would expect that at least some foregleams or intimations of it might be given. And this we find actually to be the case. "The Old Testament," says Dr. Warfield, "may be likened to a chamber richly furnished but dimly lighted; the introduction of light brings into it nothing which was not in it before; but it brings out into clearer view much of what is in it but only dimly or even not at all perceived before. The mystery of the Trinity is not revealed in the Old Testament; but the mystery of the Trinity underlies the Old Testament revelation, and here and there almost comes into view. Thus the Old Testament revelation of God is not corrected by the fuller revelation which follows it, but only perfected, extended and enlarged."[7]

The orderly, progressive way in which these doctrines are revealed, through the successive writings in the sixty-six books and over a period of approximately fifteen hundred years, is one of the strongest arguments for the Divine origin of the Bible. As all that is in the full grown tree was potentially in the seed, so we find that the clearly revealed doctrines of the New Testament were given in rudimentary form in the earliest chapters of Genesis. This is true of doctrines such as those of redemption, the Person and work of the Messiah, the nature of the Holy Spirit, and the future life. But in regard to no other doctrine is this more true than in regard to that of the Trinity. Indirect allusions to the Trinity were permitted by the Holy Spirit who presided over the writing of the books, but there is no reason to believe that the truth was apprehended in any adequate way even by the prophets themselves. The doctrine itself was veiled and held in reserve until the accompanying work of Christ in redemption made it intelligible to the human mind.

Hence the Old Testament emphasizes the unity of God and special care is taken not to aggravate the constant tendency of Israel toward polytheism. A pre-

---

7   *Biblical Doctrines*, p. 142

mature revelation of the Trinity might have been a hindrance to religious progress; for the race then, like the child now, needed to learn the unity of God before it could profitably be taught the Trinity. Otherwise it might have fallen into tritheism. Abraham in Chaldea, and the Israelites in Egypt and later in Palestine, needed to be guarded against the almost universal urge toward polytheism. The first and greatest commandment of the Decalogue was directed against polytheism, and the second and next most important was directed against idolatry with its strong tendency toward polytheism. For centuries this was drilled into the consciousness of Israel and established as a primal truth; then at long last a new day dawned, the Messiah came personally to live among and instruct His people, and the Holy Spirit was manifested in power in the early Church. The Church was then ready for the further truth that while God is One, He, nevertheless, exists as three Persons. Even after the New Testament revelation men have found it extremely difficult to state the doctrine of the Trinity without verging on Tritheism on the one hand, or Modalism or Unitarianism on the other.

PLURAL NAMES AND PRONOUNS

In the very first chapter of Genesis, as well as in many other places, we find that the names of God are in the plural, *Elohim*, also *Adonai*; and with these plural forms of the divine name singular verbs and adjectives are usually joined,—a remarkable phenomenon in view of the fact that the Hebrew language also contained the singular term *El*, meaning God. Along with the plural name, God sometimes uses plural pronouns in referring to Himself: "Let us make man in our image, after our likeness" (Gen. 1:26, 27); "And Jehovah God said,

Behold, the man is become as one of us, to know good and evil" (spoken of Adam after the fall) (Gen. 3:22); "Come, let us go down, and there confound their language" (at the tower of Babel) (Gen. 11:7); "And I heard the voice of the Lord, saying, Whom shall I send, and who will go for us?" (Isa. 6:8). In these verses we have counsel within the Trinity, God speaking with Himself. He is not taking counsel with, nor asking advice of, the angels, as some have suggested; for the angels are not His counsellors, but His servants, and, like man, infinitely below Him in knowledge. In the Divine nature itself, the Bible teaches us, is to be found that plurality of personal powers which polytheism separated and sought to worship in isolation.

The words of Moses which are so often quoted by the Jews today, "Hear, O Israel: Jehovah our God is one Jehovah" (Deut. 6:4), are in the English translation an unmeaning repetition of words, but in the original Hebrew they contain much sound instruction. "Jehovah our Elohim is one Jehovah" the word Elohim being plural shows that God the Lord, in covenant engagement and manner of existence, is more than one, yet is "one Jehovah" as regards essence of being.

The Angel of Jehovah

Very important is the fact that, beginning with the book of Genesis and continuing with ever-increasing clearness throughout the remainder of the Old Testament, we find a distinction made between Jehovah and the Angel of Jehovah who presents Himself as one in essence with Jehovah yet distinct from Him. Such an event, in which God assumes the form of an angel or of a man in order to speak visibly and audibly to man, is commonly known as a "theophany." As the revelation is unfolded by the procession of the prophets we find that divine titles and divine worship are given to this Angel and accepted by Him, that He is revealed as an eternal Being, the Mighty God, the Prince of peace, the Adonai, the Lord of David, that He is to be born of a virgin, that He will be despised and rejected of men, a man of sorrows and acquainted with grief, that He will bear the sin of many, and that he will, above all, set up the kingdom of righteousness which is to increase until it fills the whole earth. These prophecies, as the New Testament makes clear, were fulfilled in Christ, the second Person of the Trinity, who in His Divine-human capacity wrought redemption for His people and who is to rule until all enemies have been placed under His feet.

In Genesis 16:7–13 we have an account of a theophany in which the Angel of Jehovah appeared to Hagar out in the wilderness, commanded her to return to her mistress, and promised that He would multiply her seed exceedingly. Now it is clear that no created angel, speaking in his own name, could have claimed such authority. Here we are face to face with God Himself under a different manifestation; and Hagar, realizing this great truth, "called the name of Jehovah that spake unto her, Thou art a God that seeth: for she said, Have I even here looked after him that seeth me?"

In Genesis 18:1–19:29 we have a remarkable revelation of God to Abraham with the idea of the Trinity in the background. There we read: "And Jehovah appeared unto him by the oaks of Mamre...and he looked, and, lo, three men stood over against him...and when he saw them...he bowed himself to the earth, and said, My Lord (not lords), If now I have found favour in thy sight...And they said unto him, Where is Sarah thy wife? And he said, Behold, in the tent. And he

(Jehovah) said, I will certainly return unto thee when the season cometh round; and, lo, Sarah thy wife shall have a son. And Sarah heard in the tent door, which was behind him. Now Abraham and Sarah were old, and well stricken in age.... And Sarah laughed within herself.... And Jehovah said unto Abraham, Wherefore did Sarah laugh?... Is anything too hard for Jehovah?" Although the visitors appear as three men, that is, three persons, Abraham addresses them in the singular, and throughout this passage the singular references to Jehovah and the plural references to the three men are used interchangeably. And after the two "men" had gone on toward Sodom, Jehovah still stands before Abraham who pleads with Him to spare the city. Yet when the two men appear before Lot in Sodom it is Jehovah who speaks to him. "And he (Jehovah) said, Escape for thy life...And Lot said unto them (plural)...Let me escape thither (to Zoar).... And he (Jehovah) said, See, I have accepted thee concerning this thing also, that I will not overthrow the city of which thou hast spoken." In other words, Jehovah who appeared to Abraham and the three men that Abraham saw apparently were the same, and Jehovah who appeared to Lot and the two men that Lot saw apparently were the same.

In Genesis 22:1–19 we have references to God and also to one who is "the angel of Jehovah." In verse 2 God commands Abraham: "Take now thy son...and offer him there for a burnt offering," while in verse 12 the Angel of Jehovah retracts and nulllifies the command of God, with the words: "Lay not thy hand upon the lad." In verses 15–18 this angel of Jehovah swears by Himself as Jehovah, saying that He is Jehovah, and gives Abraham the promise of threefold blessing.

In Genesis 32:22–32 Jehovah appeared to Jacob under the guise of a mysterious person who wrestled with him all the night. In the morning Jacob realized that he had been face to face with God, and asked for His blessing. He called the name of the place "Peniel," "for," said he, "I have seeen God face to face."

The Angel of Jehovah appeared to Moses in the burning bush and commissioned him to go back to Egypt and deliver the Israelites. He gave Moses the promise that He would be with them and that He would lead them out (Exod. 3:1–22). In this passage the terms "God" and "Angel of Jehovah" are used interchangeably. A little later God talked with Moses on Mount Sinai and gave him the Ten Commandments. In the New Testament Stephen tells us that it was the Angel who spoke to Moses on the Mount (Acts 7:38), and Paul tells us specifically that Christ was the spiritual "rock" which followed the Israelites throughout their wilderness journey (1 Cor. 10:4).

In Ex. 23:20–23 God, speaking through Moses, promises to send His Angel before the children of Israel to keep them and to bring them into the promised land. In regard to this Angel they were especially warned: "Take ye heed before him, and hearken unto his voice; provoke him not; for he will not pardon your transgression: for my name is in him." Here we find that the Angel of Jehovah has power to forgive sins; and this in itself identifies Him with Jehovah, for we are taught that only God can forgive sins. In the New Testament we find that this power and authority belongs to the Lord Jesus Christ.

In Deuteronomy 18:18, 19 we find a most wonderful prophecy given through Moses. "I will raise them up a prophet from among their brethren, like unto thee; and

I will put my words in his mouth, and he shall speak unto them all that I shall command him. And it shall come to pass, that whosoever will not hearken unto my words which he shall speak in my name, I will require it of him." Concerning this prophecy ex-Rabbi Leopold Cohn says:

"Every Jewish scholar will admit that there has not been any other prophet like unto Moses outside of the Lord Jesus, who was even greater than Moses. That this promised future prophet is identical with the Angel of Exodus 23:21 is proven by God's command to obey Him. In addition to all these previous names and characteristics God calls Him here prophet and tells us that He will be born of a woman and be like one of our brethren. (And) notice, please, the particular punishment for disobeying this wonderful Person. 'I will require it of him.' That means that in case of Israel's disobedience to the Messiah, God is going to punish continually until they will repent and obey."[8]

In Joshua 5:13–6:3 another strange appearance is recorded. "And it came to pass, when Joshua was by Jericho, that he lifted up his eyes and looked, and behold, there stood a man over against him with his sword drawn in his hand: and Joshua went unto him, and said unto him, Art thou for us, or for our adversaries? But he said, Nay; but as prince of the host of Jehovah am I now come. And Joshua fell on his face to the earth, and did worship, and said unto him, What saith my lord unto his servant? And the prince of Jehovah's host said unto Joshua, Put off thy shoe from off thy foot; for the place whereon thou standest is holy.... And Jehovah said unto Joshua, See, I have given into thy hand Jericho, and the king thereof, and the mighty

---

8 Pamphlet, *The Trinity in the Old Testament*, p. 8

men of valour...." This "man," this "prince of Jehovah's host," whom Joshua discovered to be Jehovah Himself, is quite plainly the promised Angel who was to go before the children of Israel and lead them into the land.

In the light of the New Testament this Angel of Jehovah who appeared in Old Testament times, who spoke as Jehovah, exercised His power, received worship and had the authority to forgive sins, can be none other than the Lord Jesus Christ, who comes from the Father (John 16:28), speaks for Him (John 3:34; 14:24), exercises His power (Matt. 28:18), forgives sin (Matt. 9:2), and receives worship (Matt. 14:33; John 9:38). God the Father has not been seen by any man (John 1:18), neither could He be sent by any other; but God the Son has been seen (1 John 1:1, 2), and has been sent (John 5:36). Apart from Christ the puzzling question would be, Who can this mysterious personality be?

Indirect allusions to a complexity of persons within the Godhead are found in numerous other places. Examples are: "Jehovah saith unto my Lord, Sit thou at my right hand, Until I make thine enemies thy footstool" (Ps. 110:1), a passage which in the New Testament Christ applies to Himself (Mark 12:35–37). "Jehovah said unto me, Thou art my son; This day have I begotten thee" (Ps. 2:7), which Paul tells us was fulfilled in Christ (Acts 13:33). "Thy throne, O God, is for ever and ever" (Ps. 45:6); and the writer of the book of Hebrews tells us that this relates to Christ and His kingdom (1:8).

The fact of the matter is that the Old Testament predictions of the coming Messiah,—such as that He should be born of a virgin (Isa. 7:14), born in Bethlehem of Judea (Mic. 5:2), the son of David and heir to his throne (2 Sam. 7:12–16; Isa. 9:7), that the government should be upon His shoulder, and His name should be called Wonderful, Counsellor, the Mighty God, the Everlasting Father, the Prince of Peace (Isa. 9:6), that He should work miracles in opening the eyes of the blind, unstopping the ears of the deaf, healing the lame, and causing the dumb to speak (Isa. 35:5, 6), that He should be a man of sorrows, acquainted with grief, having no special beauty, that He should be a suffering Messiah, wounded for our transgressions and bruised for our iniquities, our substitute as a sacrifice to God (Isa. 53:1–12), that He should suddenly come to His temple (Mal. 3:1), that in His official entry into Jerusalem He should come in meekness, riding upon an ass (Zech. 9:9), etc.,—taken in connection with the descriptions of the One known as the Angel of Jehovah, were designed to make it possible for the people to recognize the Lord Jesus Christ at once by comparing these descriptions with His works, and, accepting Him, to receive forgiveness for sins.

The Holy Spirit in the Old Testament

Ordinarily the Old Testament references to the Spirit were so indistinct that they were understood to refer only to an energy or influence which proceeded from God. Nowhere is the Spirit specifically called a person; yet when He is spoken of it is in terms that may properly be applied to a person. As read in the light of the New Testament, however, there are a number of places in which He is seen to be a distinct Person. Examples are: "Who hath directed the Spirit of Jehovah, or being his counsellor hath taught him?" (Isa. 40:13); "Thou gavest also thy good Spirit to instruct them" (Neh. 9:20); "My Spirit shall not strive with man for ever" (Gen. 6:3); "Take not thy holy Spirit from me" (Ps. 51:11); "Whither shall I go from thy Spirit?" (Ps. 139:7); and in Isaiah 63:7–11 we may say that the Trinity actually comes into view, for here we have a reference to "Jehovah" who is the God of Israel and who bestows great blessings upon His people, to the "angel of his presence" who "was their Saviour," and to the "holy Spirit" who was in their midst and who was "grieved" at their rebellion. Three times He is called the "holy Spirit" (Ps. 51:11; Isa. 63:10, 11). Some theologians have understood the threefold ascription of praise in the seraphim's song, "Holy, holy, holy, is Jehovah of hosts; the whole earth is full of his glory" (Isa. 6:3), with its close parallel in the angelic chorus of Revelation 4:8, "Holy, holy, holy, is the Lord God, the Almighty, who was and who is and who is to come," as having reference to the Trinity. Certainly the divinely given formula which the priests were to use in blessing the people, "Jehovah bless thee, and keep thee: Jehovah make his face to shine upon thee, and be gracious unto thee: Jehovah lift up his countenance upon thee, and give thee peace" (Num. 6:24–26), finds its counterpart with explicit reference to the Trinity in the Apostolic Benediction of the New Testament Church: "The grace of the Lord Jesus Christ, and the love of God, and the communion of the Holy Spirit, be with you all" (2 Cor. 13:14).

Yet it is beyond question that, apart from the New Testament revelation, these intimations of the distinct personalities of the Son and of the Spirit were obscure,—and purposely so, we may say, since the people were not then ready to grasp the meaning of such a revelation. No scholars using the Old Testament alone have ever arrived at a trinitarian conception of God. In fact Jews unite with Mohammedans in accusing Trinitarians of polytheism. At New Testament times those who had been trained under the law, the Pharisees, for instance, appear to have thought of the Spirit of God and the power of God as equivalent terms.

But while not fully revealed and not recognized until Pentecost, the Holy Spirit as the executive of the Trinity was from the beginning the sustainer and moulder of the laws of nature, the One who inspired the prophets and who could be sinned against and grieved. In the second verse of the very first chapter in Genesis we read that "The Spirit of God moved upon the face of the waters," — the marginal reading says, "was brooding upon."

"Amid the darkness that surrounded the primeval chaos," says Dr. J. Ritchie Smith, "the Spirit of God is discovered, brooding upon the face of the waters, like a bird upon its nest."[9]

Just as electricity was present in nature and played a vitally important part in the lives of men long before they discovered it and learned to make it serve so many wonderful purposes, so the Holy Spirit was living and active as a distinct Person in the Godhead from eternity and moulded the affairs of men without His distinct personality being known to them.

"Even in the first chapter of Genesis," says Dr. Charles Hodge, "the Spirit of God is represented as the source of all intelligence, order, and life in the created universe; and in the following books of the Old Testament He is represented as inspiring the prophets, giving wisdom, strength, and goodness to statesmen and warriors, and to the people of God. This Spirit is not an agency, but an agent, who teaches and selects; who can be sinned against and grieved; and who, in the New Testament, is unmistakably revealed as a distinct

---

9 *The Holy Spirit in the Gospels*, p. 34

person. When John the Baptist appeared, we find him speaking of the Holy Spirit as of a person with whom his countrymen were familiar, as an object of divine worship and the giver of saving blessings. Our Divine Lord also takes this truth for granted, and promises to send the Spirit, as a Paraclete, to take His place; to instruct, comfort, and strengthen them, whom they were to receive and obey. Thus, without any violent transition, the earliest revelations of this mystery were gradually unfolded, until the Triune God, Father, Son, and Spirit, appear in the New Testament as the universally recognized God of all believers."[10]

Jewish Misunderstanding of the Doctrine

The Christian doctrine of the Trinity has been generally misunderstood among the Jewish people, with the result that they believe we worship three Gods. To set forth this idea and the reason for its strong hold on the Jewish people today we propose to quote rather extensively from the writings of one who is in a position to understand the problem,—from the writings of Ex-Rabbi Leopold Cohn. Says he:

"The reason that the Jews have become estranged from the doctrine of the Triune God is found in the teachings of Moses Maimonides. He compiled thirteen articles of faith which the Jews accepted and incorporated into their liturgy. One of them is 'I believe with a perfect faith that the Creator, blessed be His name, is an *absolute one*' (Hebrew, 'Yachid'). This has been repeated daily by Jews in their prayers, ever since the twelfth century, when Moses Maimonides lived. This expression of an *'absolute one'* is diametrically opposed to the word of God which teaches with great emphasis

---

10 *Systematic Theology*, I, p. 447

that God is not a 'Yachid,' which means an only one, or an *'absolute one,'* but 'achid,' which means a *united* one. In Deuteronomy 6:4 God laid down for His people a principle of faith, which is certainly superior to that of Moses Maimonides, inasmuch as it comes from God Himself. We read, 'Hear O Israel, the Lord our God, the Lord is ONE,' stressing the sense of the phrase 'one' by using not 'yachid,' which Moses Maimonides does, but 'achid,' which means a *united* one.

"We want now to trace where these two words, 'yachid' and 'achid,' occur in the Old Testament and in what connection and sense they are used, and thus ascertain their true meaning.

"In Genesis I we read, 'And there was evening and there was morning, *one* day.' Here the word 'achid' is used, which implies that the evening and the morning—two separate objects—are called *one*, thus showing plainly that the word 'achid' does not mean an *'absolute* one,' but a *united* one. Then in Genesis 2:24 we read, 'Therefore shall a man leave his father and his mother and shall cleave unto his wife, and they shall be *one* flesh.' Here too the word 'achid' is used, furnishing another proof that it means a *united* one, referring, as it does in this case, to two separate persons.

"Now let us see in the Word of God where that expression 'yachid,' an *'absolute* one,' is found. In Genesis 22:2 God says to Abraham, 'Take now thy son, thine *only* son.' Here we read the word 'yachid.' The same identical word, 'yachid,' is repeated in the 12th verse of the same chapter. In Psalm 25:16 it is again applied to a single person as also in Jeremiah 6:26, where we read, 'Make thee mourning as for an *only* son.' The same word, conveying the sense of one only, occurs in Zechariah 12:10, 'And they shall look upon me whom they have pierced, and they shall mourn for Him as one mourneth for his *only* son.'

"Thus we see that Moses Maimonides, with all his great wisdom and much learning, made a serious mistake in prescribing for the Jews that confession of faith in which it is stated that God is a 'yachid,' a statement which is absolutely opposed to the Word of God. And the Jews, in blindly following the so-called 'second Moses' have once more given evidence of their old proclivities of perverting the Word of the living God. The Holy Spirit made that serious complaint against them through Jeremiah the prophet, saying, 'For ye have perverted the words of the living God, of the Lord of hosts our God' (Jer. 23:36).

"This is therefore the belief of the true Christian. He does not have three gods, but 'one,' a Scriptural one, which is in Hebrew 'achid,' and which consists of three personal revelations of God as we shall see in the following Scriptures.

"In the very first verse of the Bible we find two manifestations of the Godhead. 'In the beginning *God* created...and the *Spirit of God* moved.' Here we see plainly that God taught us to believe that He is the creator of all things and that His Spirit is moving upon this world of ours to *lead, guide* and *instruct* us in the way He wants us to walk. So here in the first chapter of the Bible are *two* manifestations of God.

"It will interest the reader to know that the most sacred Jewish book, the Zohar, comments on Deuteronomy 6:4—'Hear O Israel, Jehovah our God, Jehovah is one,' saying, 'Why is there need of mentioning the name of God three times in this verse?' Then follows the answer. 'The first Jehovah is the Father above. The second is the stem of Jesse, the Messiah who is to come from the family of Jesse through David. And the third is the way which is below (meaning the Holy Spirit who shows us the way) and these three are one.' According to the Zohar the Messiah is not only called Jehovah but is a very part of the Triune Jehovah."[11]

---

[11] *The Trinity in the Old Testament*, pp. 3, 4

5. ONE SUBSTANCE, THREE PERSONS

Much of the opposition to the doctrine of the Trinity has arisen because of a misunderstanding of what it really is. We do not assert that one God is three Gods, nor that one person is three persons, nor that three Gods are one God. God is not three in the same sense in which He is one. To assert that He is would, indeed, make the doctrine what the Unitarians are ever fond of declaring it to be, mathematical absurdity. We assert rather that within the one Divine "substance" or "essence" there are three mutually related yet distinct centers of knowledge, consciousness, love and will. "Substance" or "essence" is that which the different members of the Godhead have in common, that in which the attributes and powers of Deity inhere; "person" is that in which they differ.

Yet while there are three centers of knowledge, consciousness, love and will, each of the Persons possesses *in toto* the one indivisible, incorporeal substance of Deity in which the attributes and powers inhere, and therefore possesses the same infinite knowledge, wisdom, power, holiness, justice, goodness and truth. They work together or co-operate with such perfect harmony and unity that we are justified in saying that the Triune God works with one mind and one will. What the one knows, the others know; what the one desires, the others desire; and what the one wills, the others will. Independence and self-existence are not attributes of the individual persons, but of the Triune God; hence there are not three independent wills, but three dependent wills, if we may so speak, each of which is exercised for the honour and glory and happiness of the other two.

We can illustrate the nature of the Trinity partially as follows: a bank or railroad, for instance, is owned and operated not by an individual but by many officials, stock-holders, and workers, who have a community of interests; yet we have no hesitation in speaking of the corporation in the singular and saying that the First National Bank desires to make this investment, or that the Pennsylvania Railroad is opposed to the passage of a certain piece of legislation by Congress. The decisions reached by the board of directors express the desires and purposes of the corporation as a whole. Similarly, although we believe there are three distinct Persons in the Godhead, we speak of God in the singular and apply to Him the pronouns He, Him and His.

In thinking of this mystery we are to remember that the processes of our own thinking, feeling and willing in our purely human personalities remain a complete mystery to us. It is also to be pointed out that since the incarnation Christ has also thought and felt and willed in a human manner, although the union of the Divine and the human psychological activity within the Divine-human Person, like the unity of the Persons within the Godhead, is uncomprehensible to us.

The error of the Unitarians is that while they construct a doctrine of the Divine unity they do so at the expense of the Divine personality. They look upon the Father, Son and Holy Spirit as but three successive aspects or modes in which God reveals Himself, comparable to that of a man who is known in his own family as father, in the business world as a banker, and in the Church as an elder. Such a view gives us only a modal Trinity. Any statement of the doctrine which fails to set forth both the unity and the tri-personality of the Godhead falls short of the Scripture teaching.

Since the three Persons of the Trinity possess the same identical, numerical substance or essence, and since the attributes are inherent in and inseparable from the substance or essence, it follows that all of the Divine attributes must be possessed alike by each of the three Persons and that the three Persons must be consubstantial, co-equal and co-eternal. Each is truly God, exercising the same power, partaking equally of the Divine glory, and entitled to the same worship. When the word "Father" is used in our prayers, as for example in the Lord's prayer, it does not refer exclusively to the first person of the Trinity, but to the three Persons as one God. The Triune God is our Father.

The doctrine of the Trinity cannot lead to Tritheism; for while there are three Persons in the Godhead, there is but one substance or essence, and therefore but one God. It is rather a case of the one life substance, Deity, existing consciously as three Persons. The three Persons are related to the divine substance not as three individuals to their species, as Abraham, Isaac and Jacob to human nature; they are only one God,—not a triad, but a Trinity. In the inmost depths of their being they are inherently and inescapably one.

That each of the Persons of the Trinity does possess *in toto* the numerically same substance is proved by such Scripture verses as the following: "For in him dwelleth all the fulness of the Godhead bodily" (Col. 2:9). "I and the Father are one" (John 10:30). "Believe me that I am in the Father, and the Father in me" (John 14:11). "God was in Christ reconciling the world unto Himself" (2 Cor. 5:19).

It need not surprise us that in the Godhead we find a form of personality entirely unique and different from that found in man. In the ascending scale of life as we know it in this world there are numerous modes of existence as we pass from the simpler to the more complex forms. In the plants we find what is truly called life, although it is so elementary that it does not even come to consciousness. In the insects we find sensitiveness and instinct, two particulars in which they far surpass the plant life. In the birds and animals we find affection between parent and offspring, which in some cases is very strong, together with a much higher type of instinct than is found among the insects. Man in his turn makes a tremendous advance over the animals in that he possesses reasoning power, a deep moral consciousness, and an immortal soul. These higher stages in man's nature are of course absolutely incomprehensible to the animals, birds and insects, which can, at best, have only a very vague understanding of his nature, although they fear him and recognize him as their master. Consequently we need not be surprised that the nature of God surpasses our comprehension,—that the one divine substance is conscious in three Persons, in Father, Son and Holy Spirit,—and that no attempt is made to explain that mystery to us, probably for the very reason that our little minds are utterly incapable of grasping such truth. Doubtless we are as incapable of understanding God's nature as the animals and birds are of understanding ours.

Hence it is admitted that our knowledge of the relationships which subsist between the three Persons of the Trinity extends only to the surface. There must be infinite depths in the conscious being of God to which human thought can never penetrate. We are told clearly, however, that God has existed from eternity as three self-conscious persons. Certainly we are not prepared to say that this tri-personality which has been revealed to us exhausts the mystery of the Godhead. As Dr. A. A. Hodge has well said:

"For aught we can know, in the depths of the Infinite Being there may be a common consciousness which includes the whole Godhead, and a common personality. This may all be true; but what belongs to us to deal with is the sure and obvious fact of revelation, that God exists from eternity as three self-conscious Persons, the Father, Son and Holy Spirit."

How shall we define the term "person"? As it is used in modern Psychology it means an intelligent, free, moral agent. But in setting forth the doctrine of the Trinity the Church has used the term in a sense different from that in which it is used anywhere else. The word "Person" as it is applied to the three subsistences within the Godhead, like the more important word "Trinity," is not found in Scripture itself; yet the idea which it expresses is Scriptural, and we do not know any other word that expresses so well the idea we have in mind. In the science of Theology, as in all other sciences, some technical terms are an absolute necessity. When we say there are three distinct persons in the Godhead we do not mean that each one is as separate from the others as one human being is from every other. While they are said to love, to hear, to pray to, to send, and to testify of each other, they are, nevertheless, not independent of each other; for as we have already said, self-existence and independence are properties, not of the individual persons, but of the Triune God. The singular pronouns I, Thou, He and Him are applied to each of the three Persons; yet these same singular pronoun's are applied to the Triune God who is composed of these three Persons. Hence too much stress must not be laid on the mere term. The Father, Son and Holy Spirit can be distinguished, but they cannot be separated; for they each possess the same identical numerical substance or essence. They do not merely exist alongside of each other, as did Washington, Jefferson and Franklin, but they permeate and interpenetrate each other, are in and through each other.

Consequently, in theological language we would define a person as a mode of subsistence which is marked by intelligence, will, and individual existence. The Church fathers realized, of course, that they were dealing with a doctrine which was far above the comprehension of the human mind, and, in developing the creeds, they did not attempt to explain the mystery of the Trinity, but only to state it as well as they were able with the language at their disposal. We can hope to do no more.

A Plurality of Persons Within the Godhead is in Harmony with Reason

Instead of the doctrine of the Trinity being contrary to reason as charged by Unitarians, a little considered thought should convince us that a plurality of Persons within the Godhead is eminently agreeable to reason. That there should be specifically three Persons does not necessarily follow, but that God might be more than One seems very probable. We shrink from the thought of an eternally lonely God, and take refuge in the Christian doctrine of the Trinity. This doctrine, we find, is of such a nature that, on the one hand, it avoids the hard monotheism of the Jews and Mohammedans, and on the other, the crass polytheism of the Greeks and Romans. Through the truth which it presents we are enabled to see that God has always been independent of the entire creation, that within His own nature there is to be found that absolute perfection and self-sufficiency which we instinctively ascribe to Him. Unless there is to be found that plurality of Persons within His own nature, time as well as eternity would seem to be unbearably monotonous to Him. For where among the creatures are there to be found personalities capable of responding fully to His own personality? Men and angels, while created in His image, are infinitely below Him; even the nations, Isaiah tells us, are as a drop in the bucket, and as the small dust of the balance (40:15). Only within the fellowship of the Father, Son and Holy Spirit is there to be found that full interplay of personality which the nature of God demands. And when once we have conceived of God as Trinity we can never again be satisfied with a modalistic or Unitarian conception of Him.

It has long been customary to say that the attribute of love in God proves a plurality of Persons within the Godhead, — that love is necessarily self-communicative, and that with a unitary God it could have existed only as a craving, unsatisfied, under the category of the possible rather than of the actual. This reasoning further asserts that since God is infinite His love must be infinite, and that it therefore demands an infinite object. It is usually further asserted that these two infinite Persons demand a third through whom their love is communicated and to whom it is also given. This line of reasoning, however, does not seem fully conclusive. It at least seems possible that God's own all-perfect Being could have supplied a satisfying object for His love. To say that love, in its very nature, is self-communicative, and that it therefore demands an object other than itself, seems to be merely a play on words. If we may imagine a lonely Robinson Crusoe, for instance, shipwrecked on an island for the remainder of his life, and imagine further that the storm which shipwrecked him also killed all the other persons with whom he was acquainted, would that, even as regards a limited human being, mean that the remainder of his life would be abnormal in the sense that he would be destitute of the attribute of love? Might there not be, even within his own limited nature, a kind of love based on good conscience and moral uprightness? The attribute of love need not disappear just because a person is alone. But while love in itself does not prove that there must be a plurality of Persons in the Godhead, yet what added richness, fulness and force is given to this love in either God or man when there is fellowship with others! Only thus is personality seen at its best. Hence while reason does not give us the doctrine of the Trinity in the first place, i.e., apart from revelation, it does render the negative service of showing that the doctrine is not inconsistent with other known truth, and also the positive service of showing that only on the basis of the Trinity do we have a fully adequate conception of God as self-conscious Spirit and living love.

There are, of course, elements of truth even in polytheism, distorted and perverted though they may be, and present-day men of letters, as well as philosophers in all ages and the pagan people in all nations, have found relief in speaking of "the gods."

"The most widely diffused of all religious systems," says Dr. J. Ritchie Smith, "polytheism is the perversion of a great truth, the truth of the variety and fulness of the divine nature. Lacking the conception of a God everywhere present and active, men were forced to assume a host of divinities, betweeen whom the attributes and energies of the Deity may be distributed, and who in virtue of their numbers may accomplish the works of creation and providence.... It is the distinctive mark of polytheism that it sacrifices the unity to the variety of the divine nature. Against this error the Old Testament everywhere contends. Not until it was extirpated from the minds of the chosen people, and the taint of idolatry purged away in the furnace of affliction, was the truth revealed in its fulness that polytheism strove so vainly to express. The Old Testament overthrows the error, the New Testament brings to light the truth, of polytheism.... The fulness and variety that men seek in many gods are found in one. The doctrine of the Trinity at once preserves the unity and discloses the fulness of the divine nature. God is one, is the message of the Old Testament; God is one in three Persons, is the message of the New; and the revelation is complete."[12]

---

12 *The Holy Spirit in the Gospels*, p. 19

6. Meaning of the Terms "Father", "Son", and "Spirit"

To our occidental type of mind the terms "Father" and "Son" carry with them, on the one hand, the ideas of source of being and superiority, and on the other, subordination and dependence. In theological language, however, they are used in the Semitic or Oriental sense of *sameness of nature*. It is, of course, the Semitic consciousness which underlies the phraseology of Scripture, and wherever the Scriptures call Christ the "Son" of God they assert His true and proper Deity. The term "Son" is applied to Christ, not merely as an official title in connection with the work of redemption, nor because of His incarnation or supernatural birth, nor because of His resurrection,—although in these regards He is preeminently the Son of God,—but primarily to designate an inherent trinitarian relationship. In the economy of redemption, and for the accomplishment of a specific purpose, He temporarily accepted a position subordinate to that of the Father. In its deepest sense it is a unique sonship which cannot be predicated of, nor shared with, any creature. Father and Son are co-eternal and co-equal in power and glory, partaking of the same nature and substance, and have always existed as distinct Persons. The Father is, and always has been, as much dependent on the Son as the Son is on the Father, for, as we need to keep in mind, self-existence and independence are properties not of the Persons within the Godhead, but of the Triune God.

In Hebrews 1:5–8, for instance, the writer sets forth the superiority of Christ as a Divine Person. Being Divine, or Deity, the express image of the invisible God, He is called the "Son" of God, which means precisely the same thing. He came into the world as the Son, and had existed from eternity as such. Being the Son, the One through whom the worlds were created and the heir of all things, He is declared by the writer to be God and to reign upon an everlasting throne. During the public ministry the Jews, in accordance with the Hebrew usage of the term, correctly understood Jesus' claim to be the "Son" of God as equivalent to asserting that He was "equal with God," or, simply "God" (John 5:18; 10:33); and it was for claiming to be "the Christ, the Son of God," that He was accused of blasphemy by the high priest and sentenced by the Sanhedrin to be crucified (Matt. 26:63–66).

This idea has perhaps been more clearly expressed by Dr. Warfield than by any other. Says he:

"What underlies the conception of sonship in Scriptural speech is just 'likeness'; whatever the father is that the Son is also. The emphatic application of the term 'Son' to one of the Trinitarian Persons, accordingly, asserts rather His equality with the Father than His subordination to the Father; and if there is any implication of derivation in it, it would appear to be very distant. The adjunction of the adjective 'only begotten' (John 1:14; 3:16–18; 1 John 4:9) need add only the idea of uniqueness, not of derivation (Ps. 22:20; 25; 16; 35; 17); and even such a phrase as 'God only begotten' (John 1:18) may contain no implication of derivation, but only of absolutely unique consubstantiality; as also such a phrase as 'the first-begotten of all creation' (Col. 1:15) may convey no intimation of coming into being, but merely assert priority of existence. In like manner, the designation 'Spirit of God' or 'Spirit of Jehovah,' which meets us frequently in the Old Testament, certainly does not convey the idea there either of derivation or of subordination, but is just the executive name of God—the designation of God from the point of view of His activity—and imports accordingly identity with God; and there is no reason to suppose that, in passing from the Old Testament to the New Testament, the term has taken on an essentially different meaning. It happens, oddly enough, moreover, that we have in the New Testament itself what amounts almost to formal definitions of the two terms 'Son' and 'Spirit,' and in both cases the stress is laid on the notion of equality or sameness. In John 5:18 we read: 'On this account, therefore, the Jews sought the more to kill him, because, not only did he break the Sabbath, but also called God his own Father, making himself equal with God.' The point lies, of course, in the adjective 'own.' Jesus was, rightly, understood to call God 'his own Father,' that is, to use the terms 'Father' and 'Son' not in a merely figurative sense, as when Israel was called God's son, but in the real sense. And this was understood to be claiming to be all that God is. To be the Son of God in any sense was to be like God in that sense; and to be God's *own* Son was to be exactly like God, to be 'equal with God.' Similarly, we read in 1 Corinthians 2:10, 11: 'For the Spirit searcheth all things, yea, the deep things of God. For who of men knoweth the things of a man, save the spirit of man which is in him? Even so the things of God none knoweth, save the Spirit of God.' Here the Spirit appears as the substrate of the Divine self-consciousness, the principle of God's knowledge of Himself: He is, in a word, just God Himself in the innermost essence of His Being. As the spirit of man is the seat of human life, the very life of man itself, so the Spirit of God is His very life-element. How can He be supposed, then, to be subordinate to God, or to derive His being from God?"[13]

Thus we find that the divine and original idea of fatherhood and sonship in *sameness of nature*. In the Godhead this is, of course, a purely spiritual relationship, and is in accordance with the transcendence of Deity. In the finite human sphere, where man is but a faint and imperfect pattern of God, the ideas of fatherhood and sonship, besides implying sameness of nature, imply also the ideas of origination and subordination, as well as a material nature which is mediated by sex. In the divine sphere sonship is absolute, while in the human it is relative, very much as the attributes of wisdom, power, holiness, justice and love are absolute in God but relative in man. Hence while the limitations of human language are such that we are not able to express these ideas fully, the relationship which subsists between the first and second Persons of the Trinity finds its closest analogy in the relationship which an earthly father bears to his son.

And in like manner the third Person of the Trinity, partaking of the same life substance and equal with the Father and the Son in power and glory, is called the Spirit. As the everywhere-present executive of the Trinity, immaterial and invisible, He is Spirit in the truest sense of the word. He is called the "Holy" Spirit because He is absolutely holy in His own nature, and is the source and cause of holiness in the creatures.

---

13 *Biblical Doctrines*, p. 163

We have seen that the terms "Father" and "Son" are not at all adequate to express the full relationship which exists between the first and second Persons of the Godhead. They are, however, the best that we have. They are the terms used in Scripture, and besides expressing the idea of sameness of nature, they are found to be reciprocal, expressing the ideas of love, affection, trust, honour, unity and harmony,—ideas of endearment and preciousness. When we are told that God "gave" His Son for the redemption of the world we are led to understand that the situation was in some ways analogous to that of a human father who gives his son for missionary service or for the defense of his country. It is something which involves sacrifice on the part of the father as well as privation and suffering on the part of the son. And, similarly, when the term "Spirit" is applied to the third Person of the Trinity it is not implied that His nature is in any way different from theirs, for they each partake of the numerically same substance, and are all equally spirit. He is so called, however, because He is the very life element of Deity, and because so far as our relation to God is concerned God comes to us in a spiritual way pre-eminently through this Person, His Spirit communes with our spirits, speaks to our consciences, cleanses our hearts, and leads us in right paths.

That the terms "Father" and "Son" are used in a peculiar sense as applied to the first and second Persons of the Trinity might easily be inferred from their varied usage in other parts of Scripture and in everyday speech. We read, for instance, that Jabal was the father of such as dwell in tents and have cattle, and that Jubal was the father of all such as handle the harp and the pipe (Gen. 4:20, 21). Abraham was given the promise that he should be the father of a multitude of nations (Gen. 17:4); and today every Jew regards himself as a son of Abraham. Jehovah said of the nation, "Israel is my son, my first-born" (Exod. 4:22). Of a king whose position before God is one of special honour and authority, as was that of Solomon, the Lord could say, "I will be his father, and he shall be my son" (2 Sam. 7:14). Judas was a "son of perdition" (John 17:12). We are familiar with the early Church "fathers," and we speak of one who has shown us the way of righteousness as our father in the faith. George Washington is said to have been the father of his country. The Germans speak of the fatherland, and the English of the mother country. We say that Mr. So-and-so is a loyal son of Calvin, or Luther or Wesley, and we have groups of people who call themselves Daughters of the American Revolution, or Sons of the American Legion. Hence it is quite clear that in religious as well as in secular affairs the terms father and son are used in a variety of senses.

And beyond this, although in perfect harmony with it, we find that much Scripture teaching is given in figurative language. Christ is called the Lamb of God (John 1:29; Rev. 7:14); the good shepherd (John 10:11); the door (John 10:7). He is the true vine, and His disciples are the branches (John 15:1–5); He is the true light (John 1:9); His disciples are the light of the world (Matt. 5:14), and the salt of the earth (Matt. 5:13). Similarly, God is declared to be love (1 John 4:8); light (1 John 1:5); a consuming fire (Heb. 12:29). The psalmist declares that Jehovah is his rock, his fortress, his shield and high tower (18:2), and that the righteous take refuge under His wings (91:4). When we are told that God is angry, or that He repents, or forgets, or laughs, the writer is, of course, using figurative language. Such expressions are known as anthropomorphisms, instances in which the divine action as seen from the human viewpoint is likened to that of a man who is actuated by these states of mind. These are instances in which God adjusts Himself to human language, "talking down" to us, in much the same way that human parents find it necessary to talk down to their children. We know that as a matter of fact God is altogether free from the passions and failings of human nature.

Hence in accordance with this general method of procedure it was only most fitting that the terms "Father," "Son" and "Spirit" should have been chosen to express the relationship which the first and second Persons of the Trinity bear to each other, which the third bears to the first and second, and which the first bears to us. Our language contains no terms better fitted to convey the desired meaning.

Similarly, the term "person," as we have indicated before, is but an imperfect and inadequate expression of a truth that transcends our experience and comprehension. When applied to the different members of the Godhead it only approximates the truth. It is, if you please, a make-shift, and is employed in Scripture in this sense. Yet it expresses more clearly than any other word we know the conception which the Scriptures give of the Father, Son and Holy Spirit. It is used to express an idea of personality within the Godhead which lies, we may say, approximately half-way between that of a mere form of manifestation, or personification, which would lead to Unitarianism, and the idea of fully separate, independent personalities such as is found in human beings, which would lead to Tritheism. It expresses a distinction not identical with, but in some respects analogous to, that subsisting between three different men. If there were three Gods, they would, of course, limit each other and deprive each other of Deity, since it would be impossible for each to be infinite. There is room for many finite beings, but room for only one infinite Being. The merit of the statement of this doctrine in the Athanasian Creed was that it preserved the distinct personalities and also the unity of the Godhead: "The Father is God, the Son is God, the Holy Ghost is God; and yet there are not three Gods but one God. So likewise the Father is Lord, the Son is Lord, the Holy Ghost is Lord; yet there are not three Lords but one Lord. For as we are compelled by Christian truth to acknowledge each person by Himself to be God and Lord, so we are forbidden by the same truth to say that there are three Gods or three Lords." Hence in view of the defects of human language, the very limited revelation which God has seen fit to give us concerning this subject, and the fact that the nature of this distinction must be incomprehensible to us, we are ready not only to admit, but to point out precisely, the imperfection of the language which we are obliged to employ in setting forth this doctrine.

7. Subordination of the Son and Spirit to the Father

In discussing the doctrine of the Trinity we must distinguish between what is technically known as the "immanent" and the "economic" Trinity. By the "immanent" Trinity we mean the Trinity as it has subsisted in the Godhead from all eternity. In their essential, innate life we say that the Father, Son and Holy Spirit are the same in substance, possessing identical attributes and powers, and therefore equal in glory. This relates to God's essential existence apart from the creation. By the "economic" Trinity we mean the Trinity as manifested in the world, particularly in the redemption of sinful men. There are three *opera ad extra*, additional works, if we may so describe them, which are ascribed to the Trinity, namely, Creation, Redemption and Sanctification. These are works which are outside of the necessary activities of the Trinity, works which God was under no obligation or compulsion to perform.

In the Scriptures we find that the plan of redemption takes the form of a covenant, not merely between God and His people but between the different Persons within the Trinity, so that there is, as it were, a division of labour, each Person voluntarily assuming a particular part of the work. 1st,—To the Father is ascribed primarily the work of Creation, together with the election of a certain number of individuals whom He has given to the Son. The Father is in general the Author of the plan of redemption. 2nd,—To the Son is ascribed the work of redemption, to accomplish which He became incarnate, assuming human nature in order that, as the federal head and representative of His people, He might, as their substitute, assume the guilt of their sin and suffer a full equivalent for the penalty of eternal death which rested upon them. He thus made full satisfaction to the demands of justice, which demands are expressed in the words, "The soul that sinneth, it shall die," and, "The wages of sin is death." Also, in His capacity as the federal head and representative of His people, He covenanted to keep the law of perfect obedience which was originally given to their forefather Adam in his representative capacity, which law Adam had broken and had thereby plunged the race into a state of guilt and ruin. Identifying Himself thus with His people, He paid the penalty which rested on them and earned their salvation. Acting as their King and Saviour, and also as Head of the Church which He thus forms, He directs the advancing kingdom and is ever present with His people. 3rd,—To the Holy Spirit is ascribed the works of Regeneration and Sanctification, or the application to the hearts of individuals of the objective atonement which has been wrought out by Christ. This He does by spiritually renewing their hearts, working in them faith and repentance, cleansing them of every taint of sin, and eventually glorifying them in heaven. Redemption, in the broad sense, is thus a matter of *pure grace*, being planned by the Father, purchased by the Son, and applied by the Holy Spirit.

If we may be so bold as to draw an analogy with our federal government where, when it functions normally, we have three equal and co-ordinated branches, we may say that the Father, in planning and creating the world, in ordaining its laws, and in giving to the Son a people to be redeemed by Him, corresponds to the Legislative branch; the Holy Spirit, through His regenerating and cleansing power and through His control of the minds of men and of the forces of nature, corresponds to the Executive branch; and the Son, giving Himself in the satisfaction of divine justice, and then acting as Judge of the entire world, corresponds to the Judicial branch.

Yet while particular works are ascribed pre-eminently to each of the Persons, so intimate is the unity which exists within the Trinity, there being but one substance and "one God," that each of the Persons participates to some extent in the work of the others. "I am in the Father, and the Father in me," said Jesus (John 14:11). "He that hath seen me hath seen the Father" (John 14:9). "God was in Christ reconciling the world to himself" (2 Cor. 5:19). "I will not leave you desolate: I come unto you" (through the Holy Spirit) (John 14:18). As Dr. Charles Hodge says:

"According to the Scriptures, the Father created the world, the Son created the world, and the Spirit created the world. The Father preserves all things: the Son upholds all things; and the Spirit is the source of all life. These facts are expressed by saying that the persons of the Trinity concur in all acts *ad extra*. Nevertheless there are some acts which are predominantly referred to the Father, others to the Son, and others to the Spirit. The Father creates, elects, and calls; the Son redeems; and the Spirit sanctifies.."[14]

Hence we say that while the spheres and functions of the three persons of the Trinity are different, they are

---

14 *Systematic Theology*, I, p. 445

not exclusive. That which is done by one is participated in by the others with varying degrees of prominence. The fact of the matter is that there have been three great epochs or dispensations is the history of redemption, corresponding to and successively manifesting the three Persons of the Godhead. That of the Father began at the creation and continued until the beginning of the public ministry of Jesus; that of the Son, embracing a comparatively short period of time, but the important period in which redemption was worked out objectively, began with the public ministry of Jesus and continued until the day of Pentecost; and that of the Holy Spirit began with the descent of the Holy Spirit on the disciples on the day of Pentecost and continues until the end of the age.

In regard to the work of the economic Trinity we find there is a definite procedure in the work of redemption and also in the government of the world in general, the work of the Father in creation and in the general plan for the world being primary, that of the Son in redeeming the world being subordinate to and dependent on that of the Father, and that of the Holy Spirit in applying redemption coming later in time and being subordinate to and dependent on that of the Father and of the Son. Hence in regard to the work of redemption particularly, which is the great and all-important work that God does for man in this world, there is a logical order, that of the Father being first, that of the Son second, and that of the Spirit third. And when the Persons of the Trinity are mentioned in our theological statements it is always in this order.

The Father sends the Son and works through Him (John 17:8; Rom. 8:3; 1 Thess. 5:9; Rom. 5:1), and the Father and Son work through the Holy Spirit (Rom.

5:5; Gal. 5:22, 23; Titus 3:5; Acts 15:8, 9). In Christ's own words He that is sent is not greater than he that hath sent him (John 13:16); and in His state of humiliation, speaking from the standpoint of His human nature, He could say, "The Father is greater than I" (John 14:28). Paul tells us that we are Christ's, and that Christ is God's (1 Cor. 3:23); also, that as Christ is the head of every man, so God is the head of Christ (1 Cor. 11:3). Numerous things are predicated of the incarnate Son which cannot be predicated of the second Person of the Trinity as such,—Jesus, in His human nature, advanced in wisdom (Luke 2:52), and even late in His public ministry did not know when the end of the world was to come (Matt. 24:36). In the work of redemption, which we may term a work of supererogation since it is undertaken through pure grace and love and not through obligation, the Son who is equal with the Father becomes as it were officially subject to Him. And in turn the Spirit is sent by, acts for, and reveals both the Father and the Son, glorifies not Himself but Christ, and works in the hearts of His people faith, love, holiness and spiritual enlightenment. This subordination of the Son to the Father, and of the Spirit to the Father and the Son, relates not to their essential life within the Godhead, but only to their modes of operation or their division of labour in creation and redemption.

This subordination of the Son to the Father, and of the Spirit to the Father and the Son, is not in any way inconsistent with true equality. We have an analogy of such priority and subordination, for instance, in the relationship which exists between husband and wife in the human family. Paul tells us that that relationship is one of equality in Christ Jesus, in whom "there can be no male and female" (Gal. 3:28),—woman's soul being of as much value as man's,—yet one of personal priority and subordination in which in the home and the State the husband is the acknowledged spokesman and leader. As Dr. W. Brenton Greene says:

"In the sight of God husband and wife are, and in the eye of the law ought to be, halves of one whole and neither better than the other. But while this is so and cannot be emphasized too strongly, the relationship of husband and wife, nevertheless, is such that the position of the wife is distinct from and dependent on that of the husband. This does not imply that the wife as a person is of inferior worth to her husband: in this respect there is neither male nor female; for they are both 'one in Christ Jesus.' Neither does it mean that the mission of the wife is of less importance than that of the husband. There are certain functions, moral and intellectual as well as physical, which she fulfills far better than her husband; and there are certain other functions of supreme necessity which only she can fulfill at all. What is meant, however, is that as there are some things of primary importance that only the wife can do; so there are other indispensable functions that only the husband ought to discharge, and chief among these is the direction of their *common* life. He, therefore, should be the 'head' of the 'one body' that husband and wife together form. Whether we can understand it or not, such a relationship is not inconsistent with perfect equality. It is not in the case of the Trinity. Father, Son and Spirit are equal in power and glory. Yet the Son is second to the Father, and the Spirit is second to both the Father and the Son, as to their 'mode of subsistence and operation.' Whatever, therefore, the secondary position of the wife as regards her husband may imply, it need not imply even the least inferiority."[15]

In the political realm we may say that the president of the United States is officially first, the governor of a state officially second, and the private citizen officially third. Yet they are each equally possessed of human nature, and in fact the private citizen may be a better man morally and spiritually than either the governor or the president. Also, two men of equal rank in private life may join the army, one to become a captain, the other to become a private soldier in the ranks of this captain. Officially, and for a limited time, one becomes subordinate to the other, yet during that time they may be equals in the sight of God. In the work of redemption the situation is somewhat analogous to this,—through a covenant voluntarily entered into, the Father, Son and Holy Spirit each undertake a specific work in such a manner that, during the time this work is in progress, the Father becomes officially first, the Son officially second, and the Spirit officially third. Yet within the essential and inherent life of the Trinity the full equality of the persons is preserved.

---

15 Notes on *Christian Sociology*

8. The Generation of the Son and the Procession of the Holy Spirit

The kindred doctrines of the Eternal Generation of the Son and of the Eternal Procession of the Holy Spirit are admittedly doctrines which are but very obscurely understood by the best of theologians. Certainly the present writer, with his limited study and experience, is not under the delusion that he shall be able to give a fully satisfactory explanation of them. He proposes only to define the doctrines and to offer a few brief comments.

The Eternal Generation of the Son, as stated by a representative theologian, is defined as: "an eternal personal act of the Father, wherein, by necessity of nature, not by choice of will, He generates the person (not the essence) of the Son, by communicating to Him the whole indivisible substance of the Godhead, without division, alienation, or change, so that the Son is the express image of His Father's person, and eternally continues, not from the Father, but in the Father, and the Father in the Son."[16]

The following Scripture verses are commonly given as the principal support of this doctrine: "For as the Father hath life in Himself, even so gave He to the Son also to have life in Himself" (John 5:26); "Believe me

---

16 Dr. A. A. Hodge, *Outlines of Theology*, p. 182

that I am in the Father, and the Father in me" (John 14:11); "Even as thou, Father, art in me, and I in thee" (John 17:21); "That ye may know and understand that the Father is in me, and I in the Father" (John 10:38); Christ is declared to be "the effulgence of his glory, and the very image of his substance" (Heb. 1:3); "For God so loved the world, that He gave his only begotten Son, that whosoever believeth on Him should not perish, but have eternal life" (John 3:16).

The present writer feels constrained to say, however, that in his opinion the verses quoted do not teach the doctrine in question. He feels that the primary purpose of these and similar verses is to teach that Christ is intimately associated with the Father, that He is equal with the Father in power and glory, that He is, in fact, full Deity, rather than to teach that His Person is generated by or originates in an eternal process which is going on within the Godhead. Even though the attempt is made to safeguard the essential equality of the Son by saying that the process by which the Son is generated is eternal and necessary, he does not feel that the attempt is successful. If, as even Augustine, for instance, asserts, the Father is the *Fons Trinitatis*—the fountain or source of the Trinity—from whom both the Son and the Spirit are derived, it seems that in spite of all else we may say we have made the Son and the Spirit dependent upon another as their principal cause, and have destroyed the true and essential equality between the Persons of the Trinity. As we have stated before, when the Scriptures tell us that one Person within the Trinity is known as the "Father," and another as the "Son," they intend to teach, not that the Son is originated by the Father, nor that the Father existed prior to the Son, but that they are the same in nature.

8. The Generation of the Son and the Procession of the Holy Spirit

This, apparently, was also the position held by Calvin, for at the conclusion of his chapter on the Trinity he says:

"But, studying the edification of the Church, I have thought it better not to touch upon many things, which would be unnecessarily burdensome to the reader, without yielding him any profit. For to what purpose is it to dispute, whether the Father is always begetting? For it is foolish to imagine a continual act of generation, since it is evident that three Persons have subsisted in God from all eternity."[17]

Procession of the Holy Spirit

The Procession of the Holy Spirit has commonly been understood to designate "the relation which the third person sustains to the first and second, wherein by an eternal and necessary, i.e., not voluntary, act of the Father and the Son, their whole identical divine essence, without alienation, division, or change, is communicated to the Holy Ghost."[18]

"Procession" is a more general term than "Generation," although in each case the process is admittedly inscrutable. Procession is said to differ from Generation in that the Son is generated by the Father only, while the Spirit proceeds from both the Father and the Son at the same time, — or as some have put it, proceeds from the Father, through the Son.

What we have said concerning the alleged Scripture proof for the doctrine of the generation of the Son is even more applicable to that which is advanced to prove the procession of the Spirit. There is, in fact, only one verse in Scripture which is commonly put forward

---

17 *Institutes*, Book I, Chap. 13

18 Dr. A. A. Hodge, *Outlines in Theology*, p. 189

to prove this doctrine, and it is found in John 15:26: "But when the Comforter is come, whom I will send unto you from the Father, even the Spirit of truth, which proceedeth from the Father, he shall bear witness of me." Again, the best Bible scholars are divided as to whether or not this verse teaches the "procession" of the Spirit in the sense that His Person originates as the result of an inscrutable although eternal and necessary process within the Godhead, or whether the verse merely has reference to His mission in this world as He comes to apply the redemption which Christ purchased. Jesus uses a similar form of expression when of His own redemptive mission He says, "I came out from the Father, and am come into the world: again, I leave the world, and go unto the Father" (John 16:28). In the original Greek the phrase, "came out from," which is here used of Jesus, is stronger than the "proceedeth from," which is used of the Spirit; yet the context of John 16:28 makes it perfectly clear that what Jesus said of Himself had reference to His mission and not to what is commonly termed His eternal generation; for His coming forth from the Father into the world is contrasted with His leaving the world and going back to the Father. We are, of course, told that the Holy Spirit is sent by the Father and by the Son; but the mission as He comes to apply redemption is an entirely different thing from the procession. It seems much more natural to assume that the words of John 15:26, which were a part of the Farewell Discourse, and which were, therefore, spoken within the very shadow of the cross, were not philosophical but practical, designed to meet a present and urgent need, namely, to comfort and strengthen the disciples for the ordeal through which they too were soon to pass. This was His method of teaching on other occasions, and it is at least difficult to see why He would have departed from it on this occasion. He was soon to leave the disciples, and He simply gave them the promise that another Helper, who likewise comes from the Father, shall take His place and be to them what He has been and do for them what He has done. It would seem that, since they hardly knew of the Spirit as yet, this would not at all have been an appropriate occasion to instruct them concerning the metaphysical relation which subsists between the Father and the Spirit. They are taught rather that the Spirit comes with divine authority, and that He is continually going forth from the Father to fulfill His purposes of Grace.

Hence John 15:26, at best, carries no decisive weight concerning the doctrine of the procession of the Spirit, if, indeed, it is not quite clearly designed to serve an entirely different purpose. We prefer to say, as previously stated, that within the essential life of the Trinity no one Person is prior to, nor generated by, nor proceeds from, another, and that such priority and subordination as we find revealed in the works of creation, redemption and sanctification, relate not to the immanent but to the economic Trinity.

Historically, the doctrine of the Procession of the Holy Spirit, which supposedly is of lesser consequence than that of the Generation of the Son, has been perverted and exaggerated out of all proportion to its real importance, and has been made the object of bitter and prolonged controversy between the Eastern and Western churches. It was, in fact, the immediate occasion of the split in Christendom in the eleventh century, and to this day it constitutes the main difference in doctrine between the Greek Orthodox and the Roman Catholic churches. The Greek church has maintained that the

Spirit proceeds from the Father only, while the Latin church, and also the Protestant churches generally, have maintained that He proceeds from both the Father and the Son. But certainly the evidence for the doctrine is too scanty, and its meaning too obscure, to justify the hard feeling and the ecclesiastical division which has resulted from it.

9. The Trinity Presents a Mystery but not a Contradiction

To expect that we who do not understand ourselves nor the forces of nature about us should understand the deep mysteries of the Godhead would certainly be to the last degree unreasonable. Of all the Christian doctrines this is perhaps the most difficult to understand or to explain. That God exists as a Trinity has been clearly revealed in Scripture; but the particular mode in which the three Persons exist has not been revealed. When we behold the Triune God we feel like one who gazes upon the midday sun. The finite is not able to comprehend the infinite; and the marvelous personality of the Father, Son and Holy Spirit remains and must ever remain a profound mystery regardless of all the study that the greatest theologians of the Church have expended upon it. When we try to grasp its meaning the words in Job come to mind, "Canst thou by searching find out God? Canst thou find out the Almighty unto perfection?" The question answers itself.

In every sphere we are called upon to believe many truths which we cannot explain. What, for instance, is light? What gives the force of gravity its pull, and through what medium does it act? How does the mind make contact with the physical brain?

"There are many things in the world which are true but which cannot be understood," says Dr. Floyd E. Hamilton. "What is the real nature of electricity? What is life? What enables a human body to turn the same food into bone, teeth, flesh, and hair? These are but a few of the questions which man has never been able to answer, and probably never will, but that fact does not affect their truth. They exist, and their existence does not depend upon our understanding them. In the same way, the Triune God exists and His existence does not depend upon our understanding the mysteries of His nature."[19]

And Dr. David S. Clark remarks:

"We must distinguish between apprehension and comprehension. We can know what God is, without knowing all He is. We can touch the earth while not able to embrace it in our arms. The child can know God while the philosopher cannot find out the Almighty unto perfection."[20]

"It is a mystery indeed," says Professor Flint, "yet one which explains many other mysteries, and which sheds a marvelous light on God, on nature, and on man."[21]

Most people will admit, for instance, that they do not understand Einstein's theory of relativity; yet few will be so bold as to declare it irrational. We do not understand how such a vast amount of energy can be locked up within the atom; but the recently developed atomic bomb proves beyond doubt that it is there. Unless God were too great for our full intellectual compre-

---

[19] *The Basis of Christian Faith*, p. 278

[20] *A Syllabus of Systematic Theology*, p. 59

[21] *Anti-Theistic Theories*, p. 439

hension, He would surely be too small to satisfy our spiritual needs.

But while the doctrine of the Trinity presents a mystery, it does not present a contradiction. It asserts that God is one in one respect—in substance or essence—and that He is three in an entirely different respect—in personal distinctions; and the charge of anti-trinitarians, that there is no middle ground between the Unitarian position (which asserts the unity of God but denies the Deity of Christ and the personality of the Holy Spirit) and Tritheism (which asserts that there are three Gods) is easily refuted by this fact. The doctrine of the Trinity is above reason, and could never have been discovered by man apart from divine revelation; yet it cannot be proved contrary to reason, nor inconsistent with any other truth which we know concerning God.

Furthermore, we hardly see how any one can insist that the doctrine of the Trinity strikes the average person as unreasonable when as a matter of fact Pantheism (which holds that every person and every thing which exists is but one of the innumerable forms in which God exists) is the form of philosophy which has been the most widely diffused and the most persistently held by the various peoples down through the ages. If the human mind has been able to conceive of God as existing in such an infinite number of forms, surely the statement that He exists in three Persons should not be hard to believe. The fact is that the doctrine as presented in Scripture is found to be eminently agreeable to reason. The historic Christian Church in all its branches has held tenaciously to this doctrine; and on the part of individuals the deepest and truest and most fruitful Christian faith has been found in those who have had an experimental knowledge and fellowship not only with God the Father, but also with Christ the Son and with the Holy Spirit,—that is, in Evangelicals as distinguished from Unitarians and Modernists.

Let it be remembered that we are under no obligation to explain all the mysteries connected with this doctrine. We are only under obligation to set forth what the Scriptures teach concerning it, and to vindicate the teaching as far as possible from the objections that are alleged against it. It is a doctrine which should never be presented to an unbeliever as a subject for argumentative proof, for it can be accepted only by faith, and that only after the person is convinced that God has spoken and that He has revealed this as a truth concerning Himself. With the Psalmist we are compelled to say, "Such knowledge is too wonderful for me; it is high, I cannot attain unto it" (139:6); and with Athanasius, "Man can perceive only the hem of the garment of God; the cherubim cover the rest with their wings." But though we are not able to give a full explanation of our faith we may know, and should know, what we believe and what we do not believe, and should be acquainted with the facts and truth on which our faith rests.

Many analogies have been given down through the ages to illustrate this doctrine, but we had as well admit that none of them have been of any special value and that some of them have been positively misleading. Some of the more common are: body, soul and spirit; intellect, emotion and will in man; stem, flower and seed in the plant; egg, larva and butterfly in the insect; solid, liquid and gas in matter; light, heat and radiance in the sun, etc. None of these, however, are true analogies. All of them fail to do justice to the personal element, particularly to the tri-personal element, in the Godhead. The best of them, that of intellect, emotion and will in man, presents three functions in one person, but not three persons in one substance. Those of the solid, liquid and gas, or of the egg, larva and butterfly, are not Christian, but Unitarian; for they represent the same substance as going through three successive stages.

Since there is none like God,—for "to whom will ye liken God, or what likeness will ye compare unto Him,"—we shall look in vain for any explanation of the Trinity either in the structure of our own minds or in nature about us. As the Trinity is not discoverable by reason in the first place, so it is not capable of proof by reason in the second place. We receive it only because it is taught in Scripture, and just as it is taught there. As Luther said concerning this doctrine:

"We should, like the little children, stammer out what the Scriptures teach: that the Father is truly God, that Christ is truly God, that the Holy Ghost is truly God, and yet that here are not three Gods, or three Beings, as there are three men, three angels, or three windows."

10. Historical Aspects of the Doctrine

During the first three centuries of the Christian era, theological discussion was centered almost entirely on the relationship subsisting between the Father and the Son, to the almost complete neglect of the doctrine of the Holy Spirit. In the nature of the case the development of a formal statement of the doctrine of the Trinity was a slow process. During the second and third centuries the influence of Stoic and Platonic thought caused some to deny the full Deity of Christ and to attempt to reduce Him to such dimensions as were considered commensurate with a world of time and space. Then against this tendency there arose a reaction, known as Monarchianism, which identified the Father, Son and Holy Spirit so completely that they were held to be only one Person who manifested Himself in different capacities.

We are not to infer that the doctrine of the Deity of Christ was a deduction from that of the Trinity, but rather the reverse. Because of the claims which Christ made, the authority which He assumed, the miracles which He worked, and the glory which He displayed, particularly in His resurrection, the early Christians were practically unanimous in their recognition of Him as truly God. This conviction, together with the inferential statement of the doctrine of the Trinity in the

Baptismal Formula and in the Apostolic Benediction, served as their basis in the formulation of the doctrine. But since they were equally convinced that there was but one true God, the difficulty arose as to how to reconcile these two fundamental articles of the faith. There were some who attempted to solve the difficulty by denying the Deity of Christ, but their numbers were so few during the first two centuries that they had little influence.

This controversy was settled for the early Church by the Council of Nicaea, in Asia Minor, which met in the year 325. Under the influence of Athanasius, who later became Bishop of Alexandria, the Council declared for the full and eternal Deity of Christ, who was declared to be "God of God, Light of Light, Very God of Very God, being of one substance with the Father."

But so absorbed had the Council been in working out the doctrine concerning the Person of Christ that it omitted to make any definite statement concerning the Holy Spirit. Athanasius had taught the true Deity of the Holy Spirit, but many of the writers of the period identified Him with the Logos or Son, while others regarded Him as but the impersonal power or efficacy of God. It was but natural that until the question concerning the Person and nature of the Son was settled not much progress could be made in the development of the doctrine of the Holy Spirit. The defect of the Nicene Creed was remedied, however, by the Second Ecumenical Council, which met at Constantinople in 381, and included in its creed the statement: "We believe in the Holy Ghost, who is the Lord and Giver of life, who proceedeth from the Father, who, with the Father and Son, together is worshipped and glorified, who spake by the prophets."

Another heresy which arose was that of Sabellianism. This view held that there was but one Person in the Godhead, and that the terms Father, Son and Holy Spirit simply denoted this one Person in different capacities. As Creator of the world He was known as Father; as Redeemer of the race He was known as the Son; and when working in the hearts of men He was known as the Holy Spirit. Some chose to say that it was the same God who in Old Testament times was known as Father, who afterward became incarnate as the Son, and who reveals Himself in the Church as the Holy Spirit. These different manifestations of the same Person were considered analogous to that of a man who is known in his home as father, in the Church as an elder, and in the community as a doctor.

But this view satisfied the religious consciousness of Christians in only one regard, namely, in recognizing the true Deity of Christ. Its defects were glaring; for if the phases were successive, then God ceased to be the Father when He became the Son, and ceased to be the Son when He became the Holy Spirit. The incarnation was reduced to a temporary union of the Divine and the human nature in the man Jesus Christ. This view was so out of harmony with the Scriptures that it was soon rejected, and the Church doctrine, which is neither Tritheism nor Sabellianism but the true mean between these errors, was maintained.

One other trinitarian heresy that we should notice was that of the Socinians. They held that Christ was only a man, a very good man to be sure, in fact the best of men because more fully animated and controlled by the power of God than any other had ever been, but who had no existence until he was born by ordinary generation of Joseph and Mary. They acknowledged that he possessed a more advanced revelation from God than had been given to any of the earlier prophets or teachers. They perceived the impropriety of worshipping a creature as the Arians had done, regardless of how high he might be exalted; and while less orthodox than the Arians, they were at this point more consistent. This view was, of course, condemned by the Church, but it has continued as a heresy on the outskirts of true religion down through the ages. Present-day Modernism, which is essentially a denial of the supernatural in religion, also carries on the Socinian tradition with more or less consistency.

To Augustine belongs the credit for having made a considerable advance in the development of the doctrine, and for centuries his book, *On The Trinity*, remained the standard work on the subject. While Athanasius had secured the acceptance by the Church of the true personality and Deity of the Father, Son and Holy Spirit, he did allow that the Son and the Holy Spirit were subordinate to the Father in order and dignity. Augustine did away with the idea of subordination by stressing the numerical unity of their essence, and through his powerful influence the doctrine was accepted by the Church in fact as well as in theory. Although the Reformation was a time of great advances in the development of doctrine, that of the Trinity has been wrought out so clearly at the earlier period that there was no tendency to enter into speculation concerning it. Both Luther and Calvin refused to go beyond the simple statements of Scripture, although it did fall to Calvin to reassert the self-existence and the full equality of the Son and the Holy Spirit with the Father against those who taught that the generation of the Son and the procession of the Holy Spirit denoted perpetual communication of essence from the Father and therefore dependence. In Calvin's statement the idea of the equalization of the persons took the place of the ideas of generation and procession.

The Church of the Scriptures and of the creeds is, of course, Trinitarian, not Unitarian. Up until a century ago every denomination and practically every local church taught the doctrine of the Trinity as a matter of course. But with the passing of the years a change has taken place, and even in many of the so-called evangelical churches this doctrine, which sets forth eternal and unchanging truth, is scarcely mentioned, while in others it, like many other essential truths, is challenged, doubted or denied. The truth has not changed, but the attitude of many in our generation toward that truth has changed; and today the controversy rages with new vigour, not only against the foe without, but also against the fleece-clad foe within.

In an excellent article on *The Doctrine of the Trinity*, Dr. Clarence E. Macartney has the following to say about the present-day controversy.

"What Athanasius contended against in his day was the effort to give the world a damaged Christ. He knew that a damaged Christ was no Christ. He knew that a redemption wrought out by any other save the God of redemption, God the Father, God the Son, and God the Holy Spirit, was no redemption at all. Under different names and forms there appears from time to time that same subtle effort of unbelief to persuade the world to accept a damaged Christ instead of the Christ who is the eternal Son of God. Not since the days of Arius has there been so widespread and warmly propagated a movement to substitute for the New Testament Christ, the Christ of redemption, a lesser Christ, a damaged Christ. The leaders of this movement either openly deny the New Testament accounts of the miraculous entry of Christ into the world, or hold the acceptance or the rejection of those accounts of how Christ came has nothing to do with Christianity. This new Christ probably did not work miracles. He did not die on the cross as a substitute for man, taking his place, and bearing his sins before the law of God. He did not rise from the dead with the same body in which He was entombed in Joseph's sepulchre, nor in that body did He ascend into the heavens to intercede at the right hand of God the Father Almighty; and the repeated statements of the New Testament about His glorious and triumphant return to the earth mean only that truth and right are at length to prevail upon the earth. Yet the men who hold these views still talk, and some of them still preach, about Christ. What Christ? 'Who is this?' the people exclaimed when Jesus rode into Jerusalem amid the plaudits of the multitude. Today the Christian Church may well exclaim concerning this new, this damaged Christ, 'Who is this?'"

It may be of interest to give a brief summary of the creedal statements of the Church concerning this doctrine. We have said that during the first three centuries there were no important councils and that the formulation of a creedal statement was a slow process. The early Christians held the doctrine, as it were, in solution; time and controversy were destined to precipitate it out. Because of the bitterness of the Jews, the mockery of the pagans, and the inevitable confusion and contradiction in the mode of statement even by those within the Church who honestly intended to hold what the Scriptures taught concerning it, the Church was compelled to analyse the doctrine and to set it forth in clear-cut, formal statements.

The best summary of the teaching of the various creeds, so far as we know, is found in the above-mentioned article by Dr. Macartney, and is prefaced by the following remarks:

"As we read these statements let us remember that they represent no idle and airy speculations, but a noble effort of trained minds to define and explain the truth of the Trinity as they had found it in the pages of the Bible and in the traditions of believing Christians. Let us remember, too, that these statements, especially the earlier ones, were formulated in times when Christianity was being fiercely assailed by unbelief. At Pittsburgh, St. Louis, Chicago, Detroit, and other cities of the United States, the visitor is taken to see an old fort, or the site of an old fort, where the first settlers established themselves and defended themselves. These log forts, with loophole and outlook, standing now in the midst of great cities, mark the growth and progress of the nation, for without the enterprise, heroism and sacrifice which are associated with these forts, there would not have been a nation. These ancient confessions are like venerable fortresses. They mark the crises in the history of Christianity and recall the heroism and daring of men who refused to have their Christian heritage taken from them, and in the face of a world of unbelief cried out, 'Credo! I believe!' There is nothing so ignorant, so wretched, so worthy of immeasurable scorn, as that so popular today, which belittles creeds and the men who gave them to us, and the men who defend them, and say that they have nothing to do with practical Christianity. Without these creeds, and the courage and love and faith which they represent, Christianity would long ago have perished from off the face of the earth."

1. THE NICENE CREED (325):

"We believe in one God—And in one Lord Jesus Christ, the Son of God, begotten of the Father, light of light, very God of very God, begotten, not made, being of one substance with the Father—And in the Holy Ghost."

2. THE NICENO-CONSTANTINOPOLITAN CREED (381).

In this creed the clauses concerning the Father and the Son are practically the same as in the Nicene Creed. But the article concerning the Holy Ghost is changed to the following: "And in the Holy Ghost, who is the Lord and giver of life, who proceedeth from the Father, who, with the Father and Son, is worshipped and glorified, who spake by the prophets."

3. THE ATHANASIAN CREED (ORIGIN AND TIME UNCERTAIN, BUT THE MOST LOGICAL AND ELABORATE OF THE CREEDS):

"And the Catholic Faith is this: that we worship one God in Trinity and Trinity in Unity, neither confounding the Persons nor dividing the Substance; for there is one Person of the Father, another of the Son, and another of the Holy Ghost. But the Godhead of the Father, of the Son, and of the Holy Ghost is all one; the glory equal, the majesty co-eternal. For like as we are compelled by the Christian verity to acknowledge every Person by Himself to be God and Lord, so we are forbidden by the Catholic Religion to say, There are three Gods, or three Lords."

4. THE AUGSBURG CONFESSION (1530),—THE OLDEST PROTESTANT CREED AND THE ACCEPTED STANDARD OF

LUTHERANISM:

"There is one Divine essence which is called and is God, eternal, without body, indivisible, of infinite power, wisdom, goodness, the Creator and Preserver of all things, visible and invisible. And yet there are three Persons of the same essence and power, who also are co-eternal, the Father, the Son, and the Holy Ghost."

5. THE THIRTY-NINE ARTICLES (1571),—THE CREED OF THE CHURCH OF ENGLAND AND OF THE PROTESTANT EPISCOPAL CHURCH IN THE UNITED STATES:

"There is but one living and true God. And in the unity of this Godhead there are three Persons, of one substance, power and eternity, the Father, the Son, and the Holy Ghost."

6. THE WESTMINSTER CONFESSION (1647),—THE CREED OF THE PRESBYTERIAN CHURCH, WITH WHICH THE CANON OF THE SYNOD OF DORT, THE SYMBOL OF THE REFORMED CHURCH, AGREES QUITE CLOSELY:

"There is but one living and true God. In the unity of the Godhead there are three Persons, of one substance, power, and eternity—God the Father, God the Son, and God the Holy Ghost. The Father is one, neither begotten not proceeding; the Son is eternally begotten of the Father; the Holy Ghost eternally proceeding from the Father and the Son."

11. Practical Importance of the Doctrine

The doctrine of the Trinity is not to be looked upon as an abstract metaphysical speculation, nor as an unnatural theory which has no bearing on the practical affairs of life. It is rather a most important revelation concerning the nature of the only living and true God, and of His works in the salvation of men. The very purpose of the Gospel is, of course, to bring us to the knowledge of God precisely in the way in which He has revealed Himself. And as Calvin tells us in the introductory sentence in his *Institutes*:

"True and substantial wisdom principally consists of two parts, the knowledge of God, and the knowledge of ourselves."

And then he adds that "no man can take a survey of himself but he must immediately turn to the contemplation of God in whom he lives and moves: since it is evident that our very existence is nothing but a subsistence in God alone."

The knowledge of God the Father who is the source of redemption, of God the Son who achieves redemption, and of God the Holy Spirit who applies redemption, is declared in Scripture to be eternal life. Every other conception of God presents a false god to the mind and conscience. So different is the system of theology developed, and the manner of life which flows from it, that for all practical purposes we may say that Unitarians and Trinitarians worship different Gods.

This is an advanced doctrine which was not made known in Old Testament times, and that for the very reason that it could not be understood until the objective work of redemption had been completed. But in the New Testament it is interwoven with the whole Christian economy, not in terms of speculative philosophy but in those of practical religion.

"The doctrine of the Trinity," says Dr. Bartlett, "lies in the very heart of Christian truth. It is the centre from which all other tenets of our faith radiate. If we entertain wrong views of the nature of the Supreme Being our entire theology is imperiled."[22]

Inscrutable, yet not self-contradictory, this doctrine furnishes the key to all of the other doctrines which have to do with the redemption of man. Apart from it doctrines such as the Deity of Christ, the incarnation, the personality of the Holy Spirit, regeneration, justification, sanctification, the meaning of the crucifixion and the resurrection, etc., cannot be understood. It thus underlies the whole plan of salvation. As Dr. Henry B. Smith tells us:

"For the Trinity there is a strong, preliminary argument in the fact that in some form it has always been confessed by the Christian Church, and that all that has opposed it has been thrown off. When it has been abandoned, other chief articles, as the atonement, regeneration, etc., have almost always followed it, by logical necessity; as when one draws the wire from a necklace of gems, the gems all fall asunder."[23]

---

22 *The Triune God*, p. 13

23 *System of Christian Theology*, p. 49

"The idea of the Trinity," says Dr. Warfield, "illuminates, enriches and elevates all our thoughts of God. It has become a commonplace to say that Christian theism is the only stable theism. That is as much as to say that theism requires the enriching conception of the Trinity to give it permanent hold upon the human mind—the mind finds it difficult to rest in the idea of an abstract unity for its God: and that the human heart cries out for the living God in whose Being there is that fulness of life for which the conception of the Trinity alone provides."

And again:

"If he (the believer) could not construct the doctrine of the Trinity out of his consciousness of salvation, yet the elements of his consciousness of salvation are interpreted to him and reduced to order only by the doctrine of the Trinity which he finds underlying and giving their significance and consistency to the teaching of the Scriptures as to the processes of salvation. By means of this doctrine he is able to think clearly and consequently of his threefold relation to the saving God, experienced by him as fatherly love sending a Redeemer, as redeeming love executing redemption, as saving love applying redemption.... Without the doctrine of the Trinity, his conscious Christian life would be thrown into confusion and left in disorganization if not, indeed, given an air of unreality; with the doctrine of the Trinity, order, significance and reality are brought to every element of it. Accordingly, the doctrine of the Trinity and the doctrine of redemption, historically, stand or fall together. A unitarian theology is commonly associated with a Pelagian anthropology and a Socinian soteriology. It is a striking testimony which is borne by F. E. Koenig: 'I have learned that many cast off the whole history of redemption for no other reason than because they have not attained to a conception of the Triune God'."[24]

The doctrine of the Trinity gives us a *theocentric* system of theology, and thus places in true proportion the work of God the Father. God the Son, and God the Holy Spirit. This system alone gives us the proper approach to the study of theology, showing that it must be from the standpoint of the triune God rather than from that of the second or third Person of the Trinity, or from man,—that is, theocentric rather than Christocentric or anthropocentric. It should be unnecessary for us to have to say that theocentric theology (by which we mean that which is generally known as the Reformed or Calvinistic faith) gives Christ a very high place in the system. He is the God-man, the center and course of salvation; but while soteriology has a prominent place, it is not made the organizing principle, but rather one of the subdivisions in the theological system. The history of doctrine shows quite clearly that those who have attempted to organize the system of theology around the person of Christ, regardless of their good intentions, have tended to slight other vital truths and to drift into a superficial system. Their system is unstable and tends to gravitate downward, relinquishing one doctrine after another until it becomes anthropocentric.

The third system, quite common in our day and generally known as Modernism or Humanism, is anthropocentric,—that is, it attempts to understand the nature of God by reconstructing Him from what we know of man. This system allows man to cast his own shadow over God, limiting His Lordship. It means that Christ is to be looked upon primarily as a man, and that, as expressed by an outstanding Modernist of our

---

[24] *Biblical Doctrines*, pp. 139, 167

day, nobody should go to Jesus "to his manger and his cross to find the omnipotence that swings Orion and the Pleiades." All such errors are to be avoided by placing God in His triune nature at the center of our theological system. Only thus shall we arrive at a true knowledge of Him. This is the Biblical order: first, the Father, who is the Creator and the Author of salvation; then the Son, who provides redemption objectively; and then the Holy Spirit, who applies redemption.

One cause of the strength of the Trinitarian theology has been the appeal which it makes to the inward sense of sin,—that sad weight which rests so heavily upon every serious soul,—while the great weakness of Unitarianism has been its insensibility to the reality and consequences of sin. Trinitarians have seen sin not merely as misfortune or incomplete development, but as awful and heinous crime, repulsive to God, and deserving His just wrath and punishment. They have held that it could not merely be pardoned without an atonement (that is, without any one suffering the consequences), but that God is under as much obligation to punish sin as He is to reward righteousness. On the other hand Pelagians, Socinians, and present-day Modernists and Unitarians have taken a superficial and minimizing view of sin, with the inevitable result that their faith has been superficial, their religious feelings have been deadened, and the sinews of all evangelistic and missionary effort have been cut. Having given up the doctrine of the Trinity, they naturally take a low view of the person of Christ. Even according to their own admission the great literature to which a Christian would turn for faith, hope, love and inspiration has been almost exclusively the product of trinitarian writers. Hence the best method to use in dealing with Modernists and Unitarians is to arouse in them the sense of sin; for once a person realizes the hideous and ghastly nature of his sin he also realizes that none other than a Divine Redeemer can save him from it.

And that brings us to another point: If there were no trinity, there could be no incarnation, no objective redemption, and therefore no salvation; for there would then be no one capable of acting as Mediator between God and man. In his fallen condition man has neither the inclination nor the ability to redeem himself. All merely human works are defective and incapable of redeeming a single soul. Between the Holy God and sinful man there is an infinite gulf; and only through One who is Deity, who takes man's nature upon Himself and suffers and dies in his stead, thus giving infinite value and dignity to that suffering and death, can man's debt be paid. Nor could a Holy Spirit who comes short of Deity apply that redemption to human souls. Hence if salvation is to be had at all it must be of divine origin. If God were only unity, but not plurality, He might be our Judge, but, so far as we can see, could not be our Saviour and sanctifier. The fact of the matter is that God is the way back to Himself, and that all of the hopes of our fallen race are centred in the truth of the Trinity.

It is difficult to maintain in the independence and self-sufficiency of God on any other than the Trinitarian basis. Those who believe in a uni-personal God almost instinctively posit the eternity of matter or an eternal and necessary creation in order to preserve a subjective-objective relationship. Even many Trinitarian theologians have held—whether correctly or not there is difference of opinion—that the Divine nature demands either an eternal Christ or an eternal creation. It is felt that apart from a creation a unitary God would be a most lonely and solitary Being, limited in companionship, love, mercy, justice, etc., and hence not self-sufficient. The Unitarian conception of God is unstable, and these considerations to quite a large extent account for its distinct tendency toward Pantheism. In the New England theology, for instance, we find that the high Unitarianism of Channing degenerated into the half-fledged Pantheism of Theodore Parker, and then into the full-fledged Pantheism of Ralph Waldo Emerson. As Trinitarians we feel that a God who is necessarily bound to the universe is not truly infinite, independent and free.

"A Unitarian, one-personed God," says Dr. Charles Hodge, "might possibly have existed, and if revealed as such, it would have been our duty to have acknowledged His lordship. But, nevertheless, He would have always remained utterly inconceivable to us—one lone, fellowless conscious being; subject without object; conscious person without environment; righteous being without fellowship or moral relation or sphere of right action. Where would there be to Him a sphere of love, truth, trust, or sympathetic feeling? Before creation, eternal darkness; after creation, only an endless game of solitaire, with worlds for pawns.."[25]

This Unitarian idea of God over-emphasizes His power at the expense of His other attributes, and tends to identify Him with abstract cause and thought. On the other hand the doctrine of the Trinity shows us that in His relations with us His love is primary, and that His power is exercised in the interests of His love rather than that His love is exercised in the interests of His power. The words, "God is love" (1 John 4:8) are not a

---

25 *Systematic Theology*, I, p. 127

rhetorical exaggeration, but an expression of truth concerning the Divine nature. We are convinced that the trinitarian conception of God, as judged by its piety and morality at home and its missionary zeal abroad, is by all odds the highest; and once we have thus conceived of God and felt the new fullness, richness and force given through the divine fellowship we can never again be satisfied with a modalistic or Unitarian conception.

Something of the invaluable service rendered by the doctrine of the Trinity is brought out when we see how it embraces, combines and reconciles in itself all the half-truths of the various religions and heresies that have held sway over the minds of men. There have been in the main three outstanding false systems, namely, Polytheism, Pantheism, and Deism. That these systems embrace elements of important truth cannot be denied; yet upon the whole they are false and injurious.

The truth in Polytheism, which is that God exists in a plurality of persons and powers, abundantly sufficient within His own nature to allow free play to all of the moral and social qualities or personality, is embraced in the doctrine of the Trinity; but its errors, that it destroys the unity of God, and that it separates and personifies these various powers and worships them in isolation or under some visible manifestation such as the sun, moon, rivers, trees, animals, images, etc., is rejected.

The truth of Pantheism, which is that God is everywhere present and active, the irresistible current of force which flows through all movements and all life,—a truth which, as Dr. A. A. Hodge says, "is realized in the Holy Ghost, who, while of the same substance as the Father, is revealed to us as immanent in all things, the basis of all existence, the tide of all life, springing up like a well of water from within us, giving form to chaos and inspiration to reason, the ever-present executive of God, the Author of all beauty in the physical world, of all true philosophy, science and theology in the world of thought, and of holiness in the world of the Spirit", — is embraced in the doctrine of the Trinity; but the errors of Pantheism, which are that God has no personal existence except as He comes to consciousness in man, that His only life is the sum of all creature life, and that His immediate participation in every thought and act of the creatures makes Him the author of sin, is rejected. Furthermore, in the incarnation of Christ the eternal Son God has stooped to a real and permanent incarnation, and has done sublimely what the incarnations of the heathen mythology have only caricatured.

The truth of Deism, which is that God is the Creator of the universe, the ultimate source of all power, enthroned in the highest heaven, and that His power is manifested through second causes, namely through the unchanging order of natural law, is embraced in the doctrine of the Trinity; but the errors of Deism, which are that God is an absentee God, that He works only through second causes, that He is not in personal and loving contact with His people, and that He is therefore not concerned with their prayers and desires, is rejected.

Similarly, too, in regard to the heresies which have arisen within the Christian Church. The doctrine of the Trinity acknowledges the truth of Arianism, which is that Christ existed before the creation of the world and that He was possessed of supernatural power; but it rejects the errors of Arianism, which is that Christ was not co-eternal and co-equal with the Father, that He was in the final analysis only a creature and hence far short of

Deity. With Sabellianism it acknowledges the full Deity and power of Christ and of the Holy Spirit, but denies its error, which is that it makes no proper distinctions between the Persons within the Godhead. With Nestorianism it acknowledges both the true Deity and the true humanity of Christ, but denies its error, which is that it separates the Divine and human natures in such a way as to render Him a dual personality.

Wherever the doctrine of the Trinity has been abandoned, with Christ as the connecting link between Deity and humanity, the tendency has been toward an abstract and immobile form of monotheism, toward the far-off God of Deism, or, recoiling from that, to lose God in the world of Pantheism. To identify God with nature is to attribute evil as well as good to Him; and this kind of religion had its logical outcome in the old worship of Baal, the supreme male divinity of the ancient Phoenicians, and of Ashtaroth, the goddess of love and fruitfulness, with all of their attendant and unmentionable abominations. The Christian doctrine of the Trinity supplies us with safeguards against both these errors, and at the same time provides us with the link between God and man, the link which philosophical speculation has striven so vainly to find. It is the true protection of a living Theism, which otherwise oscillates uncertainly between the two extremes of Deism and Pantheism, either of which is fatal to it.

This doctrine should, of course, be preached in every Christian Church. It is a mistake to say that people will no longer listen to doctrinal preaching. Let the minister believe his doctrines; let him present them with conviction and as living issues, and he will find sympathetic audiences. Today we see thousands of people turning away from pulpit discussions of current events, social topics, political issues, and merely ethical questions, and trying to fill themselves with the husks of occult and puerile philosophies. In many ways we are spiritually poorer than we should be, because in our theological confusion and bewilderment we have failed to do justice to these great doctrinal principles. If rightly preached these doctrines are most interesting and profitable, and are in fact indispensable if the congregation is to be well grounded in the Faith. We are convinced that the chief need of the present age is great theology, and that only the emergence and dominance of great theology will produce an adequate basis for true Christian living.

It is certain that no merely speculative theory, and especially none so mysterious and so out of analogy with all other objects of human knowledge as is that of the Trinity, could ever have held such a prominent place and been so emphasized by all of the churches of Christendom as has this doctrine unless its controlling principle were vital. In the nature of the case Anti-trinitarianism inevitably leads to a radically different system of religion. Historically the Church has always refused to recognize as Christians those who rejected the doctrine of the Trinity. Also, historically, every great revival of Christianity down through the ages has been a revival of adhesion to fullest Trinitarianism. It is not too much to say, therefore, that the Trinity is the point on which all Christian ideas and interests focus, at once the beginning and the end of all true insight into Christianity.

www.ingramcontent.com/pod-product-compliance
Lightning Source LLC
Chambersburg PA
CBHW020144130526
44591CB00030B/213